WHAT DO ECONOMISTS CONTRIBUTE?

What Do Economists Contribute?

Edited by

Daniel B. Klein

A CATO INSTITUTE BOOK

NEW YORK UNIVERSITY PRESS
Washington Square, New York

First published in the U.S.A. in 1999 by
NEW YORK UNIVERSITY PRESS
Washington Square
New York, N.Y. 10003

This book is printed on paper suitable for recycling and
made from fully managed and sustained forest sources.

Library of Congress Cataloging-in-Publication Data
What do economists contribute? / edited by Daniel B. Klein.
p. cm.
Includes index.
ISBN 0–8147–4722–1 (cloth). — ISBN 0–8147–4723–X (pbk.)
1. Economics. 2. Economists. 3. Economics—Political aspects.
4. Economics—Social aspects. I. Klein, Daniel B.
HB71.W467 1998
330—dc21   98–13820
                                                CIP

Printed in Great Britain

Contents

v

Notes on the Contributors

Ronald H. Coase was born in Middlesex, England, in 1910. Coase studied at the London School of Ecomics under Arnold Plant, who carried on the tradition of Edwin Cannan. Coase has written:

> Plant was an applied economist and his main field of interest was what today is called industrial organisation. Those of us who were associated with him were greatly interested in economic theory ... But our interest was in using this analysis to understand the working of the real economic system. Because of this, Plant, it seems to me, retained in his teaching Cannan's interest in institutions and his commonsense approach.

Coase's work is always framed as a comparison between alternative sets of real-world arrangements. His seminal work has applied this thinking to whether a firm will produce its inputs itself or buy them from other firms, whether 'neighborhood' effects are better dealt with by property rights at common law or by regulation, and whether pricing at marginal cost produces better results for society than alternative pricing schedules. He received the Nobel Prize in Economic Science in 1991. At the Nobel luncheon at the American Economic Association meetings, Coase said he felt his main achievement was helping to bring a way of thinking back to economics at the *Journal of Law and Economics* during the 1960s and 1970s.

Frank D. Graham (1890–1949) received his PhD in economics from Harvard in 1920 and taught at Princeton from 1921 until his death in 1949. His most noted professional work concerns exceptions to the doctrine of free

vii

trade, based on assumptions of increasing returns. In his memorial for Graham in the *American Economic Review* (May 19, 1950), Richard Lester wrote:

> In Graham's opinion, trained economists should exert influence in matters of public policy ... Graham's intellectual honesty and insistence on truth regardless of political currents made him seem to some a radical and to others a conservative. He attacked the wage theories of labor leaders as well as high tariffs and infringements of civil liberties; he favored ample possibilities for profitable enterprise as well as high inheritance taxes and 100-percent and commodity-reserve money. During World War II, Congressmen were astonished when he appeared at hearings to advocate higher taxes on persons like himself in order to avoid inflation. His broad economic program is most fully developed in *Social Goals and Economic Institutions* (Princeton University Press, 1943), which is one of the important works on improving the functioning of the capitalist system.

Readers may be especially interested in a three-way exchange in the *American Economic Review* (December 1947, March 1949, September 1949, and December 1949) between Graham, Lincoln Gordon, and, after Graham's death, Frank Knight.

Friedrich A. Hayek (1899–1992) studied with Friedrich von Weiser at the University of Vienna and subsequently with Ludwig von Mises in Vienna during the 1920s. Hayek's economic work lies chiefly in the theory of monetary, capital, and the trade cycle, and the theory of markets and central planning. His work built on the contributions of Mises, but Hayek cultivated a theory of knowledge that was less rationalist and more sensitive to discovery and serendipity in economic affairs. Hayek was professor at the London School of Economics (LSE) from 1931 to 1949. By the late 1930s Hayek's work moved toward broad questions of political philosophy, and he went on to regard himself not merely as a professional economist, but as a teacher and resuscitator of the then-declining philosophy of liberalism. He was the central figure in the founding in 1947 of the Mont Pelerin Society, dedicated to cultivation of liberal thought. He said the aim of liberalism 'is to persuade the majority to observe certain principles'. He was jointly awarded the Nobel Prize in Economic Science in 1974.

William H. Hutt (1899–1988) studied economics at the London School of Economics, particularly under the influence of Edwin Cannan. After his bachelor's degree in Commerce in 1924, he worked in publishing and helped to establish the British Individualist Movement, while continuing as an 'occasional student' at the LSE. In 1927 he joined the University of Capetown, first as a senior lecturer to assist Arnold Plant, and shortly afterwards as professor, remaining until 1965. He was visiting professor in the USA at Texas A & M and elsewhere from 1966 to 1981. Hutt strove to rehabilitate classical economics and to develop the theory of market coordination. Early in the 1930s Hutt defended the gold standard and vigorously maintained in several books an intellectual opposition to Keynesianism. Hutt also was acutely concerned with the economics profession as a force in society. In 1936 he published *Economists and the Public* (from which comes the Hutt selection in this volume), and in 1971 *Politically Impossible ... ?*

Israel M. Kirzner (born 1930) studied with Ludwig von Mises at New York University, where he has been a professor of economics since 1957. More than any other modern economist, Kirzner has sustained a place for entrepreneurship in economic theory, and has explored in several books the importance of discovery in market processes. A central theme of his work is that discovery factors enhance the case for the free market, but the dominant paradigms of the economics profession fail to capture and appreciate these discovery factors. His work, therefore, suggests that mainstream economics does not do justice to the case for free markets. He is considered by many to be the 'dean' of the Austrian school of economics in the United States today. Since 1977 he has led a program at New York University that trains graduate economics students in Austrian thought.

Daniel Klein (born 1962) is Associate Professor of Economics at Santa Clara University. He studied economics with an Austrian slant at George Mason University and New York University. He has written on public policy for various organisations, including the Foundation for Economic Education, the Brookings Institution, the Cato Institute, the Reason Foundation, the Independent Institute and the Institute of Economic Affairs.

Deirdre N. McCloskey (born 1942) is Professor of Economics and of History at the University of Iowa. Named Donald prior to a sex-change operation in 1996, McCloskey belonged to the quantitative movement in economic history of the 1960s and 1970s, and worked principally on nineteenth-century Britain. Since the early 1980s McCloskey has led the movement to examine the economics profession with the attitude of philosophical pragmatism. Discourse, including science, consists of rhetoric, or the art of persuasion. McCloskey examines the rhetorical techniques of economists. More importantly, McCloskey excavates the major questions of just what it is that economists are trying to persuade others of, and why. Thus McCloskey's work has led to much examination of the economics profession itself, and discussion of professional conventions that had gone largely unexamined. McCloskey says the profession has developed a refined system of specialization in research, but not upon a foundation of mutually advantageous trade among specialists. He suggests that much research is not advantageous to anyone other than the researcher.

Clarence Philbrook (1909–78) received his PhD in economics from the University of Chicago in 1947. He was

Professor of Economics at the University of North Carolina from 1947 until 1975. Aside from the article included in this volume, he published a number of thoughtful, spirited articles in the *The Southern Economic Journal* (January 1953, April 1953, October 1954, April 1957, October 1957, and January 1961); readers may be especially interested in his 'Capitalism and the Rule of Love' (April 1953). He was treasurer of the Mont Pelerin Society from 1959 to 1969. Historian of the Society, R. M. Hartwell, wrote: 'Before Philbrook, no systematic records had been kept, and Philbrook tried heroically to get the books in order.' In a letter to Milton Friedman in 1961, Philbrook wrote: 'It [the Society] plays a really significant role in keeping up the courage of many who are working in lonely surroundings.'

Thomas C. Schelling (born 1921) was for thirty years a professor at Harvard University and is now a professor at the University of Maryland. He is one of the most atypical of the great economists of the century in that he has not addressed traditional economic topics, but rather topics such as military strategy, arms control, nuclear proliferation, terrorism, organized crime, and negotiation and bargaining. In doing so, however, he developed ideas that are now applied widely throughout the social sciences. Although his main contributions have taken the form of the development of crisp, elemental ideas, he has eschewed the mathematical approaches typically used to formalize ideas. Schelling has been a (in many cases, *the*) leading pioneer in developing the following ideas: coordination problems, focal points, convention, commitments (including promises and threats) as strategic tactics, the idea that strategic strengths that may lie in weaknesses and limitations, brinkmanship as the strategic manipulation of risk, speech as a strategic device, tipping points and critical mass, path-dependence and lock-in of suboptimal conventions, self-fulfilling prophecy, repeated interaction and reputation as a basis for cooperation, the multiple self and self-commitment as a strategic tactic in the contest for self-control. Besides being a fount of seminal ideas, Schelling is widely regarded as one of the best prose stylists of the economics profession. His most famous books are *The Strategy of Conflict* (1960), *Micromotives and Macrobehavior* (1977), and *Choice and Consequence* (1984).

Gordon Tullock (born 1922) is a professor at the University of Arizona. During the 1960s, 1970s, and 1980s, at three different Virginia universities, Tullock took a leading role in turning the economist's dubious eye on the individuals in government and creating what is now known as the field of public choice. For twenty-five years he was editor of the journal *Public Choice*. Public choice is sometimes said to be simply an individual's incentive approach to government, but the Virginia style of public choice has often emphasized the exposing of government imperfection and the challenging of statist ideas. Tullock has pioneered the analysis of democratic politics, bureaucracy, and rent-seeking, as well topics in law, revolution and dictatorship. Tullock is known for defying academic convention by challenging basic assumptions.

Acknowledgments

The editor thanks the following individuals for useful comments: David Boaz, Peter Boettke, Tyler Cowen, Henry Demmert, John Majewski, and Tom Palmer.

The editor and publishers are grateful to the following for permission to reproduce copyright material as follows:

Frank D. Graham, 'On the Role of Values in the Work of Economists', a selection from *Social Goals and Economic Institutions* (Princeton: Princeton University Press, 1942).

Ronald Coase, 'Economists and Public Policy', in J. Fred Weston (ed.), *Large Corporations in a Changing Society* (New York: New York University Press, 1975); reprinted in Coase's *Essays on Economics and Economists* (Chicago: University of Chicago Press, 1994), pp. 47–63. Permission to reprint granted by New York University Press and Ronald Coase.

William H. Hutt, 'On the Decline of Authority of Economists', a selection from *Economists and the Public*, first published 1936; reprinted by Transaction Publishers, New Brunswick, NJ, 1990, pp. 34–7, 207–17.

Clarence Philbrook, '"Realism" in Policy Espousal', *American Economic Review*, 43, Dec. 1953, pp. 846–59; permission to reprint granted by the American Economic Association.

Gordon Tullock, 'How to Do Well While Doing Good!', in David C. Colander (ed.), *Neoclassical Political Economy: The Analysis of Rent-Seeking and DUP Activities* (Cambridge, Massachusetts: Ballinger Publishing Company, 1984), pp. 229–40; with permission of Gordon Tullock.

D. N. McCloskey, 'The Common Weal and Economic Stories', chapter 11 of *If You're So Smart: The Narrative of Economic Expertise* (Chicago: University of Chicago Press, 1990), pp. 150–62; permission to reprint granted by University of Chicago Press and D. McCloskey.

Thomas C. Schelling, 'What Do Economists Know?', *The American Economist*, 39, Spring 1995, 20–2; permission to reprint granted by Michael Szenberg, on behalf of Omicron Delta Episilon (publisher of *The American Economist*), and by Thomas Schelling.

Israel M. Kirzner, 'Economists and the Correction of Error', originally published as 'Does Anyone Listen to Economists?', *Inquiry*, April 1983, pp. 38–40; permission to reprint granted by Andrea Rich, on behalf of the Center of Independent Thought, and by Israel Kirzner.

Friedrich A. Hayek, 'On Being an Economist', an address given to economics students at the London School of Economics in 1944, first published in *The Trend of Economic Thinking: Essays on Political Economists and Economic History* (vol. III of *The Collected Works of F. A. Hayek*), edited by W. W. Bartley and Stephen Kresge (Chicago: University of Chicago Press, 1991), pp. 35–48; permission to reprint granted by University of Chicago Press, and by Stephen Kresge, Literary Executor, Estate of F.A. Hayek.

Every effort has been made to contact all the copyright-holders, but if any have been inadvertently omitted the publishers will be pleased to make the necessary arrangements at the first opportunity.

'[It] was at the same time a tract for the times, a specific attack on certain types of government activity which Smith was convinced, on both a priori and empirical grounds, operated against national prosperity.'

— Jacob Viner, 'Adam Smith and Laissez Faire', *Journal of Political Economy*, April 1927, pp. 198–232

'Adam Smith thought that, "to expect, indeed, that freedom of trade should ever be entirely restored in Great Britain is as absurd as to expect an Oceana or Utopia should ever be established in it". Yet seventy years later, largely as a result of his work, it was achieved.'

— F. A. Hayek, *Law, Legislation and Liberty*, vol. I (Chicago: University of Chicago Press, 1973), p.65

1 Introduction: What Do Economists Contribute?

Daniel B. Klein

The essays gathered here speak of the choices economists make. Which subjects to write on, which premises to follow, which authorities to appeal to, which methods to use, which tones to assume, which audiences to address, which challenges to respond to, which social purposes to serve: all these choices are made each time an economist acts as an economist. Are economists today, in making their individual choices, led to promote ends of human betterment? Most of the present authors suspect that much choosing by economists is not for the better.

Economists are quick to find flaws in markets, governments, and other institutions. Yet they rarely aim their flaw-finding at their own professional institutions (not publicly, anyway). In such matters, their public attitude is rather like their attitude toward their children: acceptance without critical examination. Some economists harbor doubts about normal professional practice and standards, doubts confined to private thought and discreet conversations. A few, such as Arjo Klamer, David Colander, Thomas Mayer, Deirdre McCloskey, and Lawrence Summers express their doubts publicly.

The impetus for the present volume stems from the belief that academic institutions are failing and that they take a dim view of certain research activities which do advance the sound practice of political economy. If so, economists might find that pressures to pursue academic work divert them from contributing to the art and science of political economy. They are torn between doing well

1

and doing good. The present volume has been assembled in the hope that it will find its way into the private chamber of the academic economist. It is meant to suggest that the economist really does face a tension between doing well and doing good. The existence of such a tension is addressed especially by the selections from Frank Graham, Ronald Coase, William Hutt, and Clarence Philbrook. The dates of those articles, as well as the allusions they make to Frank Knight, Edwin Cannan, and others, indicate that economists have for generations protested certain barren tendencies of doing well academically. It is also hinted at in Gordon Tullock's more upbeat article (written during the early 1970s). The selections from Deirdre McCloskey, Thomas Schelling, Israel Kirzner, and Friedrich Hayek also deal with the parts economists play in the cause of human betterment.

Each chapter has its own important points, and sometimes they have points in conflict. But in the main they converge. Taken together these essays offer a statement about economics as a profession, and a vision of the economist's responsibility. Here I raise a series of key ideas from the various contributions.

THE PRACTITIONER OF POLITICAL ECONOMY IS THE EVERYMAN

Hutt and Hayek point out a major difference between political economy and such disciplines as physics, chemistry, engineering and medicine. For these latter disciplines, experts are appointed to make important decisions. Practitioners in those fields are therefore confident that basic learning will be used to improve the conditions for human beings. In political economy, however, the practitioner is not the expert economist, but every public official and ordinary voter; the Everyman. The practitioner of political economy is typically highly ignorant of basic economic ideas. 'The result,' says Hayek (pp. 137, 133), 'is that in economics you can never establish a truth once and for all but have always to convince every generation anew'. Economists as a group do not succeed in continued inculcation of basic ideas (ideas that professional economists might see as 'inframarginal'). Consequently, in this field, 'almost more than any other, human folly displays itself'. That the practitioner of political economy is the Everyman places the professional economist in a dilemma: Should he strive to enlighten the practitioner of political economy by teaching the basics, in the manner, say, of Frederic Bastiat or Henry Hazlitt? If so, will it pay off in professional esteem and security? If the academic profession rewards, rather, paradigmatic study addressed merely to other academics, how does the economist who responds accordingly justify his salary? Can he find a responsible belief that doing well professionally is also doing good for society?

ELEMENTAL IDEAS FORSAKEN

Many of the authors in this book suggest that because the practitioner is the Everyman, elemental economic ideas and simple policy solutions are forsaken in public affairs. Coase (pp. 39, 35) says, 'the advice we do have to offer which would be valuable, if followed, consists of a few simple truths ... What is discouraging is that it is these simple truths which are so commonly ignored.' Graham (p. xvi) similarly says that economic policy has fallen far short of attainment of 'clearly desirable, and patently realizable, ends'. Hayek (p. 136) notes that 'knowledge once gained and spread is often, not disproved, but simply lost or forgotten'. Indeed, Coase quotes similar remarks from Frank Knight, Edwin Cannan, and Adam Smith. The essays indicate that there is a tradition within economics of coping with the practitioner dilemma and striving to keep elemental ideas alive in public discourse, generation after generation.

If the authors feel that elemental ideas and simple solutions are being forsaken, they must have in mind specific ideas and solutions. Most of the authors feel that government policy should move significantly in the direction of private property and freedom of contract. We can be sure that all of the authors, save Schelling and perhaps Graham, would agree that in America today government spending should be reduced, perhaps gradually, by at least 50 percent and regulation by at least 75 percent. But the most basic message of the volume does not depend on libertarian policy views. It depends only on the belief that elemental ideas, whatever one believes them to be, would better reach the Everyman if economists focused more on public policy and took greater part in public discourse.

Although the authors mainly concur on policy reform, it is doubtful that they would agree fully on the 'simple truths' of the discipline. Perhaps all would cite economic principles as taught in introductory courses: mutual gains, the division of labor, opportunity cost, marginal utility, incentives, competition, comparative advantage, transaction costs, and so on. Surely all would favor stories of human wants creating, within a property rights system, opportunities for people to gain by satisfying those wants. Surely all would favor stories of decentralized coordination of economic activities. Writers in the Austrian tradition, including Hayek, Hutt, and Kirzner, might also include discovery of opportunity, entrepreneurship, and the diffuseness of knowledge. Tullock and others may be keen to include, among the elements of political economy, analysis of incentives in government. McCloskey might emphasize the role of speech in economic activities. Schelling emphasizes the importance of accounting identities for the economic system. Thus, even where opinions concur on how policy should be reformed, minds differ as to which elementals ideas should be stressed as *the arguments in support of* those policy reforms.

ECONOMISTS CAN INFLUENCE PUBLIC AFFAIRS

George Stigler, though at an earlier time apparently sanguine about economists' coming influence as policy advisors (see the quotation on pp. 43–4 below), is quoted by Kirzner as follows: 'Economists exert a minor and scarcely detectable influence on the societies in which they live' (Stigler, 1982, 63). Stigler (p. 34) tells economists not to preach to the Everyman. He even asserts that economists have nothing of interest to tell the Everyman. The Everyman knows his interest and optimizes in searching for information. Stigler tells economists they might as well focus on academic pursuits.

The present authors (with the qualified exceptions of Hutt and Hayek), in contrast, urge economists to take greater part in public discourse. They affirm economists' influence in public affairs. Tullock says economists played a major part in the deregulation of trucking, airline, and banking and the reduction of tariffs. McCloskey (p. 167) says, 'Ideas, not dollars, conquered the regulatory agencies'. Philbrook speaks of 'idea force': '[H]owever an idea may get into a mind, it is capable of dying there or of gathering immense force. Moreover, a number of minds can be seeded with one expression of the idea. Potentially, then, the force may grow at an astronomical rate' (Philbrook, p. 83).

Perhaps the hopefulness of the authors stems in part from an intuition about the nature of knowledge. If knowledge were merely information (as Stigler often seems to suggest), then there is good reason to be fatalistic. Individuals have effective incentives to search for the bits of information, such as a telephone number, which they lack; further information thrust upon them by economists is unlikely to influence them. But knowledge is not merely information; it is also interpretation and judgment. The Everyman may sometimes demand information used to get pork from his congressman. But the Everyman has a steady, if limited, demand for socially-relevant economic interpretation and economic opinion. That demand is serviced by union leaders, business spokesmen, environmental activists, so-called consumer advocates, lawyers, lobbyists, media pundits, politicians, bureaucrats, and economists. By providing powerful interpretation and scrupulous judgment, economists can take a more vital role in public discourse.

Tullock says citizens would have opposed the Civil Aeronautics Board (CAB) all along if they had known the cartel interpretation of the arrangement. McCloskey says that sports metaphors such as 'U.S.-versus-Japan' damage economic understanding, and alternative interpretations of mutual gains and comparative advantage advance understanding. Coase cites an example of thought experiment – imagining the incentives faced by an official at the Food and Drug Administration (FDA) in deciding whether to approve a new drug – as an interpretation with great persuasive power. The knowledge offered in these cases is not principally information – facts and figures – but rather interpretations: stories, histories, thought experiments, and metaphors.

Whereas Stigler, cherishing the notion that knowledge is merely information, eradicates the very idea of error in social events (see, for example, Stigler 1976), Kirzner (1979) insists that error is pervasive in economic processes, and he similarly applies the idea to public affairs. Error may be corrected when the individual discovers a new interpretation: knowledge includes not only information, but also *insight*: insight, that is, to new and superior interpretation. Kirzner criticizes Stigler for failing to incorporate a notion of error into his economics and into his public philosophy. Other authors side with Kirzner and speak of economists helping people to discover the error of their ways. Philbrook (p. 75) speaks of the economist-adviser helping 'others discover correct attitudes'. Schelling (p. 123–4) speaks of 'free lunches all over just waiting to be discovered' by economists proposing policy reforms.

And the knowledge-as-merely-information view suppresses a third facet of knowledge: judgment. When interpretations are multiple the individual has to decide which to take stock in. Judgment is the facet of knowledge where ideas are not merely recognized, but believed and used. Judgment is revealed in action and captured most expressly in phrases such as, 'I feel we should do such-and-such'. As Michael Polanyi (1962) explained, there is an element of commitment in believing, in the sense that one's beliefs partly determine how one thinks, what one does, and who one is. This is the moral dimension of knowledge, affecting what it is that one will stand for. Economists can influence the Everyman not only by providing facts and interpretations, which help him see where his interest lies, but also by providing moral guidance about what his interests *should be*. Rhetoric scholars from Adam Smith to McCloskey recognize that persuasive authority flows from the *ethos* of the speaker. When an economist argues against licensing restrictions, the argument persuades not only because it is cogent and factually supported, but also because it is sincere and because it is an economist's. 'Economists claim to see around and underneath the economy. They claim to do the accounts from the social point of view' (McCloskey, p.158). An economist urges deregulation of business and persuades others that he comes to that conclusion not because he is pro-business but because he is pro the entire society. For this reason, an earnest conversation with an economist can alter one's values. McCloskey refers to the 'moral authority' of regulatory commissions infiltrated by economists. Philbrook (p. 850) also speaks of exerting influence by making evident 'the validity of a value'.

Economists can offer valuable information, interpretations, and judgment. A fuller appreciation of the nature of knowledge may lead economists to reject fatalistic thinking that says whatever is is efficient. They may instead adopt an attitude expressed by Aaron Wildavsky (1988, 91): 'It is up to the wise to undo the damage done by the merely good'. The merely good make errors, errors that economists can correct.

And even if the influence of economists is small, that small influence is precious. As Coase (pp. 44, 51) puts it: 'An economist who, by his efforts, is able to postpone by a week a government program which wastes $100 million a year (what I would consider a modest success) has, by his action, earned his salary for the whole of his life'. Coase encourages economists to take part in public discourse, not because he believes their influence to be large, but because 'even a modest success is not to be despised'.

UNPOPULARITY, SORROW, AND THE STRUGGLE AGAINST DESPAIR

Although the authors express hope that economists will influence public affairs, several tell why the hope must be tough and deep-reaching. The economist's good works rarely bear fruit in any direct way. The economist's advice seems to fall on deaf ears. When good advice is rejected, the rejection is brusque and ignorant. Even in the rare case when the advice takes root, the sage's influence is long lost and he receives no credit. For the most part, participation in public discourse is like tutoring an ornery and spoiled child. The economist must plead to get attention; once he has attention, his appeals consist of elementary ideas rehearsed earnestly and painstakingly, and illustrated by imaginative stories and examples. Just when he thinks the public and policymakers are taking his precepts to heart, they suddenly abandon his instruction and for no good reason. His only recourse is to keep on hoping and pleading. The whole effort is thankless and may make one ridiculous.

A sense of frustration, even desperation, comes across especially in the early pieces by Hutt, Graham, and Hayek, written during the 1930s and 1940s when statism, both as public policy and as intellectual force, was advancing rapidly. Hayek suggests that economic reasoning is likely to lead to conclusions in conflict with universal human instincts and simplistic visions of a happy society. Indeed, we see in this address from 1944 the kernel of ideas that Hayek developed over the subsequent four decades, ideas about the tension between the values of traditional society and the desirable rules for modern society. Hayek (p. 146) cautions his young-economist auditors that in economics 'the ruthless pursuit of an argument will lead you almost certainly into isolation and unpopularity'. The economist 'must not look for public approval or sympathy for his efforts'. Hutt's counsel is equally dispiriting. He says that the libertarian-oriented economist must 'be aware of a periodic recurrence of a sense of utter helplessness':

> On all sides he thinks he sees the survival of ignorance and confusion of thought on matters which affect human welfare; and he feels that nothing that it is within his power to do or say can have the slightest effect in checking the accumulation of wrong ideas and false policies which they bring forth. He recognizes that in spheres in which policy and action can be influenced, he is doomed to virtual dumbness to-day. He does not attempt the impossible. He seldom protests, for experience and history have taught him that protests are without avail and merely damaging to his reputation. He realizes that persistent opposition to the popular illusions of his time will simply bring him the notoriety of a crank. (Hutt, p. 53)

The sense of frustration and despair is greatest for those economists who take part in public discourse. One of Hutt's section headings reads: 'It is as a critic of actual affairs that the economist is most aware of his ineffectiveness'. Although statist thinking has, in recent decades, not continued to advance the way it did when Hutt wrote, and although Milton Friedman has had no apparent difficulty in remaining cheerful in his conversation with the public, the fundamental problems described by Hutt and Hayek remain highly pertinent to libertarian economists today.

THE GREAT ESCAPE: FROM PUBLIC DISCOURSE TO ACADEMIC CRAFTS

Hutt (p. 55) continues by describing how the economist working on applied issues responds to the frustration: 'In practice, then, he also confines his efforts mainly to writing books and articles that are read only by other economists, and to attempting (if he is a teacher) to disseminate understanding to successive groups of students who come under his influence'. Hutt builds a bridge from the fundamental problems that economists experience in public discourse to the problems within economics as an academic profession. This bridge is less explicit in the other chapters, but many of them show deep concern with the failures of economics as an academic profession. The chapters, therefore, explore the problems an economist faces in two different realms: that of public discourse and that of academic pursuits. Hutt suggests a sociological theory that bridges the two realms, a theory implicit in several of the other chapters.

Hutt clearly identifies the turn inward – into the academy, into strictly economist-to-economist discourse – as an *escape* from the frustration of public discourse. (This theme had been framed earlier and in pungent terms by Cannan, Hutt's teacher; see Cannan, 1933.) The academic pursuit he identifies with this escape is 'pure theory,' or model building: 'The economist may devote himself to "pure theory," where he escapes from the sense of frustrated effort' (Hutt, p. 54). Graham (p. 31) also regards economists' 'logical gymnastics' as an 'intellectual retreat from a disillusioning contemplation of the march of events'.

The rationale for this escape is that 'such an economist will correspond to the "pure scientist" in other fields' (Hutt, p. 54). This presumption of 'science' brings a set of professional norms and standards, with stated ideals of 'value freedom,' 'objectivity,' 'positive analysis,' and 'scientific method'. But, as Wayne Booth (1974) has argued, the collection of such precepts turns out to be mutually dependent, not independently grounded. Science is the conforming to accepted scientific methods. Science is what scientists say it is, and scientists are those who do science. The science talk amounts to a faith in favored professional institutions and practices. That faith may be a worthy one; the point is that economists often do not recognize that it is one interlocking set of beliefs, and do not critically examine it on a broader plane. As Thomas Kuhn (1977, xxi) says, 'The hypotheses of individuals are tested, the commitments shared by his group being presupposed; group commitments, on the other hand, are not tested, and the process by which they are displaced differs drastically from that involved in the evaluation of hypotheses.'

Those turning inward, therefore, do not think of it as an escape. Rather, they defend the turn inward on the grounds that science (that is, doing well academically) has its own pace and force. In the long run, advancing science will do more for society than will direct engagement with the public. This is precisely how Stigler (1982, 34, 67; 1988, 85, 179) justifies the turn inward.

However, the legitimation of the turn inward is based on an erroneous and largely unexamined faith in academic institutions, a faith that I will refer to as 'the Great Faith'. As Hutt, Graham, Hayek, Philbrook, Coase, Tullock, Kirzner, and McCloskey each indicate in their own way, the fact that the practitioner of political economy is the Everyman means that the field must remain fundamentally different from the natural sciences. The profession proceeds on tacit presumptions about what 'it is all about,' but those presumptions are fundamentally wrong. Graham writes:

> Economics has always been under suspicion as a 'science,' and the consequent defensive attempts on the part of its exponents to force their theory into rigid scientific forms has frustrated its application to the facts of life. (Graham, p. 28)

> Much first-rate analytical skill and much scholarly industry has miscarried because the road to academic recognition lay in the refinement of traditional technique, or in assiduous dust-gathering, with little consideration of ultimate purpose. The means have been exalted over the end, and the neophyte, compelled to show his mastery of technique, has quickly learned to love and practice it for its own sake. (Graham, p. 29)

VARIETIES OF PARADIGMATICISM

The Great Faith depends on a strong set of academic standards and practices, which become the markers of 'true science'. In other words, the Great Faith is a faith in dominant formal modes of scholarly discourse, or paradigms (Kuhn 1970, 10–11; 1977, xviii–xx). While a paradigm is a formal mode of scholarly discourse, another term is needed to mean a strong and rigid allegiance to paradigm. Wishing for a less ugly alternative that would do the job, I adopt *paradigmaticism*. (An alternative term might be *formalism*, but that term does not adequately convey the allegiance to paradigm, which need not be mathematical.) Paradigmaticism is what many of the authors find wrong with the economics profession. Many see a conflict within economics between a public-discourse orientation and paradigmaticism. Explicitly or otherwise, the present authors (with the qualified exception of Hayek) protest against paradigmaticism in the profession, because they feel that it diverts economists from assisting the true practitioner of political economy.

The leading form of paradigmaticism is undue stress on formal model-building, and is explicitly protested here by Graham, Hutt, and Philbrook. In their other writings, Hayek, Coase, Kirzner, and especially McCloskey have done likewise. Another form of paradigmaticism protested here by Coase and Philbrook is undue stress on empirical work according to favored quantitative methods (nowadays, regression analysis). And Graham's (p. 28) allusion to the assiduous fact-gathering of Institutionalism perhaps indicates a past form of paradigmaticism.

CONFLICT BETWEEN PARADIGMATICISM AND RELEVANCE

The Everyman does not think or talk the paradigm. Anything valuable that paradigmatic discourse teaches, therefore, must be relayed in a language that the Everyman understands. Although Graham, Hutt, Coase, Kirzner, and Hayek express appreciation for the fruits of paradigm, most of the authors feel that the paradigmatic spirit is too strong, and that the findings of mainstream research are too often not worth transmitting to the Everyman. The objection is not categorical; it is an issue of whether economists are too far down the paradigmatic end of the production frontier.

The Great Faith maintains that paradigmaticism best serves society, that doing well professionally is doing good. But the authors point out conflicts between paradigmaticism and economic enlightenment. Of quantitative paradigms, Coase writes:

> But this development is not without its costs. It absorbs resources which might otherwise be devoted to the development of our theory and to empirical studies of the economic system of a nonquantitative character. Aspects of the economic system which are difficult to measure tend to be neglected. It diverts attention from the economic system itself to the technical problems of measurement. (Coase, p. 45)

Graham directs more biting remarks at formal model-building (written in 1942!):

> Theory has, at length, become so 'scientific' and abstract as to intrigue the mathematicians who have taken delight in developing the concept of a kaleidoscopic and frictionless play of atomistic units in a complex and eternally unfolding equilibrium. The notion of equilibrium suggested equations; equations are prolific parents of their kind; and the game has gone on until the pages of the more esoteric economic journals have become a mass of hieroglyphics intelligible only to those who know the code. All the inconvenient freight of fact has been discarded by the more recondite practitioners until the 'science' has come to move in a

realm of pure abstraction useful for purposes of cerebration but of steadily declining practical importance.
(Graham, p. 28)

In a similar vein, Hutt inveighs:

Our own suggestion is that whilst the impressive developments in the logical structure of Political Economy
which the last forty years have witnessed are valuable
contributions to the physiology of economic method,
they have tended, in their treatment by some of the
most fertile methodological inventors, seriously to
obscure the persistent relevance of the backbone of the
science. (Hutt, p. 65)

Hutt criticized certain remarks on method made by Joan
Robinson, and he identifies a key implicit and undefended
conviction of the Great Faith: that knowledge is not true
science until it has been captured in a formal model. That
conviction justifies the denigration and dismissal of other,
less paradigmatic, kinds of research (such as those kinds
associated with the collected authors). But Hutt (p. 62)
challenges this conviction: 'Because the theorists of the
mathematical and diagrammatical schools are in some
cases unable to find realistic categories with which their
method can satisfactorily deal, that does not prove that
other means of so doing do not exist'. As McCloskey has
argued at length, model-building is just one genre of
metaphor making. There is no reason to suppose that it is
the only useful one, and there is good reason to believe
that it is incapable of capturing many important theoretical ideas and is unsuitable for many theoretical purposes.

PARADIGMATICISM INHIBITS THE
CULTIVATION OF ECONOMIC JUDGMENT

The following chapters suggest that paradigmaticism
inhibits the cultivation of economic judgment in the

professional economist. Indeed, before one becomes an economist, one is merely the Everyman. And after becoming an economist one remains also the Everyman, since one continues to be subject to nonprofessional cultural and intellectual influences. Addressing young economists, Hayek tells of our having convictions before we come to economics:

> It is probably still true of most of us – and in this, too, economics differs from most other subjects – that we did not turn to economics for the fascination of the subject as such ... The fact which we must face is that nearly all of us come to the study of economics with very strong views on subjects which we do not understand. And even if we make a show of being detached and ready to learn, I am afraid it is almost always with a mental reservation, with an inward determination to prove that our instincts were right ... Nothing is more pernicious to intellectual honesty than pride in not having changed one's opinions – particularly if, as is usually the case in our field, these are opinions which in the circles in which we move are regarded as 'progressive' or 'advanced' or just modern. You will soon enough discover that what you regard as specially advanced opinions are just the opinions dominant in your particular generation. (Hayek, pp. 138, 139)

Implicit in Hayek's discussion is his belief that the cultivation of good judgment in economics is a process of coming to understand why free, voluntary, private activities are much more socially effective than government enterprise and regulation. The average college student today has not undergone this learning process. Rather, he is a citizen of a society where conventional thinking is highly statist. People are accustomed to pervasive government with its institutions, rituals, personalities, histories, permanence, and incomparable power. Government as a binding, guiding force for society is a central idea and value in Western culture. The average college student has been schooled by government employees and gets his or her ideas from news services that depend greatly on the cooperation of government officials. There is a good chance his or her parents work for government.

The process of cultivating good economic judgment entails the rigorous probing of major public-policy issues. The probing is audacious in its imagination and vision, and ruthless with conventional thinking. It is highly argumentative and personally challenging. It studies the arguments on all sides of the issue. The issues are genuine and the positions are genuinely held by mentors. Students acquire judgment by being expected to develop convictions; not because having convictions is desirable, but because the process of developing convictions impels a scrupulous awareness of what the arguments are and a searching understanding of how the arguments really stack up. A sound training in economics is a process of edification.

The problem with paradigmaticism is that it thwarts the edification process. Advanced courses in model-building and econometrics can in no way substitute for an impassioned, searching study of the FDA, drug prohibition, occupational licensing, antitrust policy, and the US Postal Service. Such study relies, to be sure, on quantitative evidence and careful reasoning based on models, but, as many mainstream economists have noted, the evidence and reasoning with the most 'oomph' are very low tech. Hutt explains the consequences of paradigmaticism:

> [T]he swamping of economic treatises with mathematics has ... diverted attention from fundamentals to points of analytical interest, and incidentally thereby led to some actual corruption or unjustifiable weakening of basic tenets ... [The intricacies of the mathematical method] appear to have caused some of those practising it to lose their continuous intimacy

with *certain broad unquestionable elements of reality which ought always to dominate in applied theory*. Whilst not actually inducing generalizations from special cases, some economists seem to have given undue stress to *curiosa* in a manner that has tended to distort their *judgment* and weaken the authority of economists generally. (Hutt, p. 57, first set of italics added)

Where Hutt refers to 'certain broad unquestionable elements of reality,' we might especially consider the pervasiveness of yet-to-be-discovered opportunities and the radical decentralization of knowledge, themes prominent in the tradition of Smith and Hayek. Yet it is precisely these themes that the model-building paradigm suppresses.

McCloskey (p. 108) writes of the breakdown of judgment in economics: 'Economics around 1950 gave up social philosophy and social history to become a blackboard subject ... [W]hy should historical and philosophical doubts that the wealth [of nations] arises from planning be entertained if a sweet diagram can prove that planning works?' Economists trained only in paradigm simply do not have an opportunity to cultivate economic judgment.

Hutt (p. 63) explains that the problem then spills over to the public at large: 'the public mind would be led away from basic essentials ... owing to the diffusion of effort ... to ingenious futilities'. Paradigmaticism undermines economists' authority with the Everyman, first, by inhibiting the cultivation of good judgment and thereby reducing wise consensus among economists, and, second, by leading economists to pursue irrelevant questions and speak an esoteric language. Economists turn their back on the Everyman, and the Everyman turns his back on economists. It is this breakdown in authority, a breakdown in economics as a moral and intellectual force against *dirigisme*, that several of the authors see as the great tragedy of modern economics.

CYNICISM AND ACCEPTANCE OF THE STATUS QUO

The attitude of some market-oriented economists brings to mind a parable from Søren Kierkegaard:

> It is said that two English noblemen were once riding along a road when they met a man whose horse had run away with him and who, being in danger of falling off, shouted for help. One of the Englishmen turned to the other and said, 'A hundred guineas he falls off'. 'Taken,' said the other. With that they spurred their horses to a gallop and hurried on ahead to open the tollgates and to prevent anything from getting in the way of the runaway horse. In the same way, though without that heroic and millionaire-like spleen, our own reflective and sensible age is like a curious, critical and worldly-wise person who, at the most, has vitality enough to lay a wager. (Kierkegaard 1978, p. 15)

Many economists see the great power of economics both to find viable solutions and to convince others, yet nonetheless feel no responsibility to make economics sing in the body politic. If judgment within the profession is to be improved and the authority of the profession enhanced, the first task is to get economists with good judgment to work together. There is a rift within the more libertarian-oriented half of the profession, a rift over paradigmatic work versus nonparadigmatic, policy-relevant work. The paradigmatic comrades sometimes slight nonparadigmatic work as 'nonscience' and policy work as 'advocacy'. They usually have (or hope to have) opportunity in prestigious academic circles. They are sometimes caught between two conflicting personal goals: winning academic esteem and favor, and winning ideological esteem and favor.

The turn inward often triumphs. Though not advancing ideas in opposition to wise policy, the economist abandons his ideological interests and neglects research topics that could advance wise policy. He justifies his choices with the notion that advancing science does more good, ultimately, than does 'advocacy,' and science is 'value neutral'. But as Graham (p. 30) says, '[t]he assertion that the scientist should be completely free of value judgments, even if it were realizable, is in itself, of course, a value judgment'. The trouble is not that, at bottom, implicit value judgments are, after all, snuck in; the trouble is that the implicit value judgments are unexamined, and turn out to be unworthy. Graham wryly exposes the weakness of the inward faith: '[Some] writers have been content to affirm that science is concerned only with means and not with ends and that the final determination of ends must be left to those fitted to make value judgments, *whoever they might be*'. (Graham, p. 32; italics added). Graham's statement could be read with George Stigler in mind; Stigler (1982, 3) writes: 'Economists have no special professional knowledge of that which is virtuous or just.'

Graham suggests that the inward turn must rest on a belief that the academic system is driven by intelligent forces and beneficial mechanisms, and that economists, like grocers, will best serve society by taking consumer tastes ('ends' in Graham's language) as given, playing their part quiescently in the vast division of labor, and getting on in their careers. But economists have not, of course, actually done the economics that would be necessary to support such a view of their own 'industry'. Again, the problem is not that economists are going on faith and making value judgments – such is ineluctable – but that the implied faiths and judgments are so ill-considered.

Graham's sarcastic *whoever they might be* zeros in on the error. The social ends that economists are presented with are not determined by experts in such a task, but by our collective foolishness as democratic society. Here the 'consumer' is not choosing wisely. The 'consumer' is the Everyman, who ignorantly and negligently makes the real choices in political economy. To believe that there is an efficacious connection between what is decided by referees at the prestigious academic journals to what should be known by the Everyman-practitioner is truly a great faith.

Several of the articles suggest that the acceptance of the status quo is really a fleeing of responsibility. Often the rationales for the profession's norms are lacking or half-hearted, and cynicism is rife. The authors dislike this trend. Their response is clear: *whoever they might be* might as well be us, economists. It is up to the wise to undo the damage done by the merely good.

Graham argues that it is not enough for economists to understand how the status quo operates. If economists are to lead society toward better things, they must explore 'things as they could and ought to be' (Graham, p. 31). Economics, says Graham (p. 30), 'must be not only analytical but imaginative'. An example from the modern literature comes to mind: there is a proliferation of technical articles that analyze particular aspects of modern central banking systems, but relatively scant attention is given to the question of whether central banking should exist in the first place, and of how a *laissez-faire* system of banking would work. Work that posits major policy reform and explores how such regimes might work in practice are often disparaged as 'nonscience,' 'nonrigorous,' 'speculative,' and 'unrealistic'.

PHILBROOK'S COUNTERATTACK AGAINST THE 'REALISTS'

Clarence Philbrook evidently had been derogated for lacking 'realism' one too many times. His article, published in the *American Economic Review* in 1953, responds to the charge of 'unrealism' that one suffers when proposing or merely exploring major policy reform, such as *laissez-faire* banking. The article is pithy and difficult, and some introductory remarks may be helpful.

Imagine an economist presenting research on how *laissez-faire* banking would work, and arguing in its favor. His colleagues do not seriously consider his arguments, but simply say the whole notion is 'unrealistic' and dismiss the research as 'advocacy'. But the critics do not explain what they mean by 'unrealistic,' nor how the charge justifies their dismissal. Philbrook searches for the implicit justification of the 'realism' criterion, and then answers it. Thus, he has the job of scrupulously articulating his opponents' argument and then knocking down that argument.

Philbrook's opponents, the 'realists,' are not model builders, but rather applied economists working on institutional and policy topics. Perhaps the 'realists,' says Philbrook, take the view that everything in society should be taken as given and unalterable. But the very act of conducting research and giving advice must proceed on at least a pretense that some pieces of the situation may be subject to influence by the economist-adviser. Otherwise, there would be no point to the whole enterprise. Philbrook (p. 74) notes that any policy change requires 'a change of attitudes on the part of a large number of persons'. Thus, short of confessing to charade, 'realists' must join Philbrook in presuming that economics is capable of influencing citizens and public officials, if only remotely.

The 'realism' philosophy must, therefore, come down to a set of beliefs about which policy reforms are politically viable and which are not. It must rest on a set of beliefs about the probabilities associated with various reform proposals. Free banking, for example, however desirable it may be thought to be, is regarded to have such a small probability of realization that it is foolish to even discuss it, and hence is dismissed as 'unrealistic'. Or, Philbrook says, 'realists' might have in mind a criterion that mixes the realization probability with the degree of desirability of the reform. 'Men called "unrealistic" are those who disregard this principle and presumably those who assign probability weights incorrectly' (Philbrook, p. 79). When reading Philbrook, bear in mind from the start that he rejects the entire probability philosophy which he attributes to the 'realists'. His own view is that professional esteem and rewards should not be withheld from economists who study the desirable, regardless of its probability of being realized.

Philbrook's counterattack is rich and multifaceted. One point of his valiant essay deserves special attention. The probability that free banking, for example, will be realized depends on how many other economist-advisers advocate the reform. 'If all, however, follow the "probability" principle, no one can commit himself until many others (nearly all?) have committed themselves'. If making their choices simultaneously, economists' advice will 'be the product of infinite involutions of guesses by each about what others are guessing about what he is guessing about what they will advocate' (Philbrook, p. 84). Philbrook is pointing out that if science is what scientists say it is, and scientists are those who practise science, then scientists are playing a coordination game with bad equilibria. One equilibrium in particular stands out for its focal properties. Philbrook (p. 86) writes of the 'mutual anticipation ending only in universal support of the status quo'. The focal power of the status quo shapes the evolution of professional ('scientific') norms. The profession suffers from what path-dependence theorists call 'lock-in'. Philbrook (p. 71) remarks: 'There has grown a widespread practice of cooperation with "things as they are," without explicit criticism of them, which is bound to have the effect of active approval regardless of whether such is intended'. Empirical economists tease out regression results about the status quo, but neglect candid comparison with major policy reform – abolition of the FDA, the Securities and Exchange Commission (SEC), government schools, government roads, etc. – even though such reforms may be thought desirable. Philbrook's article is aimed at applied economists who pull their punches with status-quo policies, in the name of 'positive analysis,' 'realism,' 'science,' etc.

WHAT, SPECIFICALLY, ECONOMISTS SHOULD DO MORE OF

With the qualified exception of Hutt and Hayek, the authors encourage economists to become more engaged in public discourse. This means efforts at general education – Tullock suggests talking to Rotary Clubs and writing newspaper articles – or it might mean writing as adviser to policy makers, or it might mean simply focusing one's work more on public-policy issues. All these activities are likely to be less paradigmatic than what now prevails as normal professional work. Since the practitioner of political economy is the Everyman, however, one could argue that these activities advance the art more than does highly paradigmatic work.

Most of the authors feel that economists have gotten carried away with paradigm. Most favor an adjustment at the margin toward less paradigmatic, more policy-oriented work. Such an adjustment would not be without its difficulties and drawbacks. Indeed, the great virtue of paradigmaticism is that it provides relatively clear criteria for rating research. Academic affairs call for a set of standards which can, relative to other possible standards, be applied consistently, to reduce vexing internecine conflict over every orals examination, job candidate, or tenure case. Without common standards and values an academic community is not a community. Paradigmaticism prevails precisely because it serves these institutional functions. Tempering the stress on paradigm – by giving more credit in promotion cases, for example, to general-readership articles, think-tank reports, and lectures to Rotary Clubs, and less credit to articles in prestigious journals – could lead to a less definite set of standards and less predictable decision making. Academic economists should find the marginal rate of transformation that maximizes not their own comfort and sanctuary, but the service economics renders to society.

DOING WELL CAN MEAN DOING GOOD

Gordon Tullock's lecture, 'How to Do Well While Doing Good!', was first written for a seminar at Virginia Polytechnic Institute some time during the early 1970s (it remained unpublished for more than a decade). He says virtue does not have to be its own reward. Talking to Rotary Clubs can pay off professionally. Maybe things were different in the early 1970s, or maybe Tullock is disguising the facts to serve a greater good. Tullock (p. 92) in fact belies his upbeat promise of professional payoff when he describes what he proposes as 'unprofessional'.

The real point is that economists should do good sometimes regardless of professional considerations. Tullock says:

> Even if there were no beneficial impact on your career, nevertheless, I would urge it on you … It is likely that you will do more good for the world by concentrating on abolishing some [wasteful government] organization in your locality than the average person does – indeed, very much more. It is an unusual form of charity, but a form in which the payoff would be high. (Tullock, p. 102)

Similarly, Schelling (p. 124) concludes his address to the Economics graduating class at Berkeley: 'To those of you who become professional economists I urge you: get out there and help find those free lunches.' All of the authors esteem economists who bring economic enlightenment to the Everyman. Doing so may not help you to do well professionally (it may even hurt); however, some find knowing that they would have their esteem to be well-doing of another sort.

References

Booth, Wayne C. 1974. *Modern Dogma and the Rhetoric of Assent* (Chicago: University of Chicago Press).

Cannan, Edwin. 1933. 'The Need for Simpler Economics', *Economic Journal*, 43 (September), pp. 367–78.

Coase, Ronald H. 1975. 'Economists and Public Policy', in J. Fred Weston (ed.), *Large Corporations in a Changing Society* (New York: New York University Press). Reprinted in Coase's *Essays on*

Economics and Economists (Chicago: University of Chicago Press, 1994), pp. 47–63, and in the present volume.

Graham, Frank D. 1942. *Social Goals and the Economic Institutions* (Princeton, NJ: Princeton University Press). Selection (from pp. xv–xx) reprinted in the present volume.

Hayek, Friedrich A. 1944. 'On Being an Economist', an address given to economics students at the London School of Economics in 1944, first published in *The Trend of Economic Thinking: Essays on Political Economists and Economic History* (vol. III of *The Collected Works of F. A. Hayek*), edited by W. W. Bartley and Stephen Kresge (Chicago: University of Chicago Press, 1991), pp. 35–48. Reprinted in the present volume.

Hutt, William H. 1936. *Economists and the Public* (reprinted New Brunswick, NJ: Transaction Publishers, 1990). Selection (from pp. 34–7, 207–17) reprinted in the present volume.

Kierkegaard, Søren 1978. *Parables of Kierkegaard*, edited by Thomas C. Oden (Princeton, NJ: Princeton University Press).

Kirzner, Israel M. 1979. *Perception, Opportunity, and Profit: Studies in the Theory of Entrepreneurship* (Chicago: University of Chicago Press).

Kirzner, Israel M. 1983. 'Does Anyone Listen to Economists' (a review of George Stigler's *Economist As Preacher and Other Essays*), *Inquiry*, April, pp. 38–40. Reprinted with new title in the present volume.

Kuhn, Thomas S. 1970. *The Structure of Scientific Revolutions*. 2nd edn (Chicago: University of Chicago Press).

Kuhn, Thomas S. 1977. *The Essential Tension: Selected Studies in Scientific Tradition and Change* (Chicago: University of Chicago Press).

McCloskey, D. N. 1990. 'The Common Weal and Economic Stories', Chapter 11 of *If You're So Smart: The Narrative of Economic Expertise* (Chicago: University of Chicago Press), pp. 150–62. Reprinted in the present volume.

Philbrook, Clarence 1953. '"Realism" in Policy Espousal', *American Economic Review*, 43 (December), pp. 846–59. Reprinted in the present volume.

Polanyi, Michael 1962. *Personal Knowledge: Towards a Post-Critical Philosophy* (Chicago: University of Chicago Press).

Schelling, Thomas C. 1995. 'What Do Economists Know?', *The American Economist*, 39 (Spring 1995), pp. 20–2. Reprinted in the present volume.

Stigler George J. 1976. 'The Xistence of X-Efficiency', *American Economic Review*, March, pp. 213–16.

Stigler, George J. 1982. *The Economist as Preacher and Other Essays* (Chicago: University of Chicago Press).

Stigler, George J. 1988. *Memoirs of an Unregulated Economist* (New York: Basic Books).

Tullock, Gordon 1984. 'How to Do Well While Doing Good!', an address delivered during the early 1970s at Virginia Polytechnic Institute. Published in David C. Colander (ed.), *Neoclassical Political Economy: The Analysis of Rent-Seeking and DUP Activities* (Cambridge, Mass.: Ballinger, 1984), pp. 229–40. Reprinted in the present volume.

Wildavsky, Aaron 1988. *Searching for Safety* (New Brunswick, NJ: Transaction Publishers).

2 On the Role of Values in the Work of Economists*

Frank D. Graham

Man's reach, we may hope, will always exceed his grasp, and heaven, therefore, even if we are all alike, is unattainable. Men must therefore pursue, rather than expect, happiness, and, rather than happiness, they might better follow some slightly less evanescent wills-o'-the-wisp.

Human goals lie vaguely on a distant horizon whose margin fades forever as we move. But it is of supreme importance that we move along the appropriate road. That road is rocky but we shall find no magic carpet which will avoid the necessity of our traveling it.

This book is based on the thesis that the road we must travel is the road of power-*cum*-freedom. The general locus of its subject is the vaguely defined area which is common to ethics, politics, and economics. The territory was once familiar ground but it has, in recent decades, been much neglected. Specialization in subjects of study has carried the day and been pressed to such extremes that the necessity for coordination has had few to serve it. This is peculiarly true in the field of applied economics. It is, perhaps, in that field that we have fallen farthest short of attainment of clearly desirable, and patently realizable, ends. This is in no small degree the outcome of the diversion, if not the perversion, of the effort of students of economic affairs.

---

* This selection is taken from the Introduction of Graham, *Social Goals and Economic Institutions* (Princeton, NJ: Princeton University Press, 1942), pp. xv–xx.

Orthodox economic theory is in part a description of what is, or was, and in part a 'purification' of the system it purports to describe. Economics has always been under suspicion as a 'science,' and the consequent defensive attempts on the part of its exponents to force their theory into rigid scientific forms has frustrated its application to the facts of life. Not only have postulates, which originally represented an approach to reality, been progressively 'refined,' and thereby made less real, but the persistent trend of economic institutions has been away from the forms for which the doctrines were, in the first place, cast. Economic theory and economic fact have been marching in opposite directions.[1] Theory has, at length, become so 'scientific' and abstract as to intrigue the mathematicians who have taken delight in developing the concept of a kaleidoscopic and frictionless play of atomistic units in a complex and eternally unfolding equilibrium. The notion of equilibrium suggested equations; equations are prolific parents of their kind; and the game has gone on until the pages of the more esoteric economic journals have become a mass of hieroglyphics intelligible only to those who know the code. All the inconvenient freight of fact has been discarded by the more recondite practitioners until the 'science' has come to move in a realm of pure abstraction useful for purposes of cerebration but of steadily declining practical importance.

The Institutional school arose in revolt from this technique, and even the later mathematical economists, recognizing the barrenness of their earlier method, have sought to enlarge their premises but have not succeeded in giving them greater reality. The Institutionalists deplore the deductive approach, but their own studies have, in the field of policy, proved as abortive as has orthodox theory, largely because they, in common with the orthodox neoclassical school, have sought to keep their discipline free of value judgements (*Wertfrei*).[2] Devoid of any, even a bad, unifying principle, they have been assiduously collecting facts without any teleological value. Their very effort to achieve an impossible objectivity has made their work jejune. This is even more true of the historical school which has devoted enormous energy to a largely feckless research.

Much first-rate analytical skill and much scholarly industry has miscarried because the road to academic recognition lay in the refinement of traditional technique, or in assiduous dust-gathering, with little consideration of ultimate purpose. The means have been exalted over the end, and the neophyte, compelled to show his mastery of the technique, has quickly learned to love and practice it for its own sake.

This is not to deny the virtue, even the necessity, of abstract speculation or the desirability of the most catholic comprehension of the facts. It is merely to assert that these should be tools rather than ornaments and that we should never cease to ask ourselves what we want and how we propose to get it.

To the contentions of the enthusiasts for *Wertfreiheit* it must be conceded that a large objectivity is, of course, a necessary condition of scientific inquiry. This does not mean, however, that the scientist must be free from all emotion or from preference for any given set of ends. It may, indeed, be confidently asserted that perfect objectivity, in the sense of freedom from emotion and from more or less conscious judgments of the relative values of different ends, is impossible. Complete objectivity can be attributed only to materials and machines, but men are, inevitably, something more or less than these. Thinking is necessarily subjective and conditioned by nonrational impulses.

All rational activity, and therefore all scientific ratiocination and experimentation, is purposive; that is, such activity is guided by some preconceived end which the thinker uses as an arbitrary norm to determine what thoughts, actions, and data are relevant. In science, the only question which arises out of the problem of the selection of goals or ends is whether these aims are to spring from mere curiosity or from a desire to discover relationships which may be of value to preconceived purposes.

Whatever be the source of choice which leads one scientist, apparently in a spirit of mere curiosity, to study economics, another physics, and still others mathematics, there can be no doubt that the decision to choose one field rather than another rests on a value judgment.

It makes no necessary difference to the pursuit of a scientific inquiry what ends are posited and whether they are posited by some outside authority or are laid down by the seeker himself. In the latter case they are, of course, likely to correspond with inevitable emotional preferences which may distort the vision. It is on the probability that this is so that the case for so-called *Wertfreiheit* rests. But the proponent of *Wertfreiheit* is subject to a psychological quirk at least as likely to affect his judgment as are the predilections of the student frankly interested in the ends he seeks to realize. The person who believes himself entirely free of value judgments is a victim of self-delusion and, under the influence of unconscious bias, is perhaps more prone to error than the person who, conscious of his preference, is watchful that he does not indulge in wishful thinking.

The assertion that the scientist should be completely free of value judgments, even if it were realizable, is in itself, of course, a value judgment. There seems, moreover, to be no a priori reason for the contention that it is better to be cold than warm. On the contrary, a convincing case could be made for warm feelings and a cool choice of methods for their satisfaction. Science involves both analysis and synthesis and the synthesis must be purposive to some ulterior end. Science, and particularly social science, must be not only analytical but imaginative. The goal must be not exclusion of one or the other requirement but their maintenance in separate compartments of the mind so that they do not corrupt one another by miscegenation. Insistence on *Wertfreiheit*, therefore, boils down to nothing more than a caution against a refusal to face facts. About this there is no room for any controversy.

The great classical economists were not chary of choosing express or implied objectives nor, on this account, afraid of the charge of lack of scientific objectivity. The degree of governmental action or inaction which they favored, and indeed the whole body of their thought, was inspired by the desire and design to promote freedom, equity, and a rapidly progressive mastery of the physical basis of living. They knew that the conditions under which life, and work, is carried on are quite as important as a part of the standard of living as the immediate return on such work as is performed, and that no economic system can be satisfactory if it traverses the fundamental desires of the majority of its members.

The tradition of Adam Smith, and of John Stuart Mill, is more fruitful than that of the rigid and frigid Ricardo, however necessary Ricardianism may be in preventing prejudiced, confused, or merely wishful thinking. Political economy, perhaps in contrast with 'economics,' is concerned not only with things as they are but with things as they could and ought to be. The latter implies either an acceptance of whatever is as right, and a mere explanation of the facts, or a set of predefined ends toward which the facts are, as far as possible, to be shaped. Mill was acutely conscious of the gap between the real and the ideal and was concerned, above all else, to narrow it, but, to his heirs in economic speculation, logical gymnastics have 'offered an ... intellectual retreat from a disillusioning contemplation of the march of events'.[3] They therefore resigned the role of philosopher and took refuge in a neutrality under which, in place of inquiries into the wealth of nations, 'we are ... offered explanations of what will happen (once equilibrium has been finally reached) when we choose each of the several alternatives which are commonly thought available to that end'.[4] The final retreat was into a sanctum sanctorum from which the dictum went forth that 'economics' has nothing to do with the actual conduct of what is still (no doubt perversely) called economic life.

Slightly less impeccably objective writers have been content to affirm that science is concerned only with means and not with ends and that the final determination of ends must be left to those fitted to make value judgments, whoever *they* might be. Any technique of social control, however, involves human interests and the exercise of power over men. This means that any suggestion of a method for the solution of a social problem is shot through with normative implications. There can be no practical divorce, in social analysis, of means and ends when the results of such analyses are to be utilized in the attempt to effect any change in an existing situation. The only honest course, then, is the declaration of a scheme of social values as a basis for the development of suggestions with respect to social institutions.

Notes

1.   Cf J. M. Keynes in the introduction to D. H. Robertson's *Money* (New York: Harcourt, Brace & Company, 1929), p. v, where he says that the 'Theory of economics does not furnish a body of settled conclusions immediately applicable to policy. It is a method rather than a doctrine, an apparatus of the mind, a technique of thinking, which helps its possessor to draw correct conclusions'. But not, be it noted, with respect to policy. Keynes, moreover, in this passage, fails to distinguish economic theory from pure logic where it has been well said that we never know what we are talking about or whether what we are talking about is true, that is to say, that all purely logical statements are tautologies. The whole content of economic theory, if Keynes has given us a good definition, may be summed up in the phrase 'tautological transformations'.
2.   Despite his Olympian attitude this was not true of Veblen, but Veblen was father, rather than representative, of Institutionalism.
3.   A. S. J. Baster, *Advertising Reconsidered* (London: P. S. King & Son, 1935), p. 83.
4.   *Loc. cit.*

3 Economists and Public Policy*

Ronald H. Coase

The large enterprise that I will be examining is the study of economics, and the performance that I will be appraising is not that of corporations but of my colleagues in the economics profession. The particular aspect of their work that I will be examining will be the part that economists play in the determination of public policy.

I know, of course, that there are some economists who argue that economics is a positive science and that all we can do is to explain the consequences that follow from various economic policies. We cannot say whether one policy is preferable to another, because to do so would require us to introduce value judgments, in the making of which we have no special competence. Thus we can say that certain agricultural policies (say collectivization) will lead to widespread starvation, but we cannot say whether collectivization is or is not desirable. Such self-restraint is I think unnecessary. We share (at least in the West) a very similar set of values, and there is little reason to suppose that the value judgments of economists are particularly eccentric. There will, of course, be instances in which, knowing the consequences of a change in policy, there will be differences in opinion as to whether the change is desirable. But such cases are, I believe, exceptions, and can be treated as such. I agree with Milton Friedman's judgment that:

* First appeared in J. Fred Weston (ed.), *Large Corporations in a Changing Society* (New York: New York University Press, 1975). Reprinted in Coase, *Essays on Economics and Economists* (Chicago: University of Chicago Press, 1994), pp. 47–63.

33

currently in the Western World, and especially in the United States, differences about economic policy among disinterested citizens derive predominantly from different predictions about the economic consequences of taking action – differences that in principle can be eliminated by the progress of positive economics – rather than from fundamental differences in basic values, differences about which men can ultimately only fight.[1]

Of course, if this is so, it has the result that an analysis of the consequences of alternative social arrangements becomes a prescription for policy (since we all share the same values). Thus it hardly matters, once it is established that a certain policy will lead to widespread starvation, whether we add that the policy would be undesirable, although to refrain from doing so on principle seems like an affectation. In general, one would expect that a statement of the consequences of alternative policies would bring its policy recommendations with it.

Whether they should or not, few economists do in fact refrain from making pronouncements on public policy, although the state of the economy (both here and elsewhere) suggests either that the advice given is bad or, if good, that it is ignored. Of course, there is the other possibility, more disturbing from some points of view but reassuring from others, that the advice is disregarded, whether it is good or bad. I happen to think that we are appallingly ignorant about many aspects of the working of the economic system, at least so far as that part of economics is concerned in which I am particularly interested: the economics of the firm and industry. I think we know very little about the forces which determine the organization of industry or the arrangements which firms make in their transactions with one another. We have, of course, been told that when we consider the economics of the system as a whole, what is termed macroeconomic policy, that things are very different, at least since the appearance of Keynes's *General Theory*, and that we now know how to secure full employment coupled with a stable price level. I leave to others more knowledgeable in this field whether our present troubles are due to ignorance, impotence in affecting policy, or some other cause. But I do seem to have detected in recent years a degree of humility among workers in this field not hitherto observed.

Yet having said this, I would not wish to argue that economists do not have something valuable to contribute to the discussion of public policy issues. The problem is that economists seem willing to give advice on questions about which we know very little and on which our judgments are likely to be fallible, while what we have to say which is important and true is quite simple – so simple indeed that little or no economics is required to understand it. What is discouraging is that it is these simple truths which are so commonly ignored in the discussion of economic policy.

It requires no great knowledge of economics to know that at a lower price, consumers will buy a greater quantity. Or to know that as the price falls, producers will be willing to supply less. Even the combining of these two notions to show that, if the price is put low enough, producers will not be willing to supply as much as consumers wish to buy (so that what is called a 'shortage' will result) is easy enough to understand. Indeed, the essentials of such a situation would be understood by many who have not studied economics at all. Yet consider an example. In the early 1960s, the Federal Power commission began to regulate the field price of natural gas. The price was frozen at the 1959–60 level. It became apparent that this was lower than the price would have been without regulation. What followed was what one would expect. Consumption was encouraged; the discovery and exploitation of natural gas was discouraged. The effect of the regulation was at first masked by the short-term fall in the cost of coal and by a reduction in the quality of what was supplied (the consumer had less assurance of the availability of the gas in future). But as time went on, the nature of the regulation-induced shortage of natural gas (to use Paul MacAvoy's phrase) became obvious to the meanest intelligence, and the Federal Power commission began to take steps to raise the price.

A number of studies have been made (by MacAvoy and others), and there is general agreement about what happened. One of these studies was carried out by Edmund Kitch at the University of Chicago Law school and was published in the *Journal of Law and Economics* in 1968.[2] Later Kitch decided that it would be a good idea if he updated his study. He then presented his findings in Washington, DC, in 1971 in a talk entitled 'The Shortage of Natural Gas'.[3] Much of the audience consisted of Washington journalists, members of the staff of congressional committees concerned with energy problems, and others with similar jobs. They displayed little interest in the findings but a great deal in discovering who had financed the study. Many seem to have been convinced that the law and economics program at the University of Chicago had been 'bought' by the gas industry. In fact, this study had not been financed by any organization of any kind connected with the gas or oil industries. But a large part of the audience seemed to live in a simple world in which anyone who thought prices should rise was pro-industry and anyone who wanted prices to be reduced was pro-consumer. I could have explained that the essentials of Kitch's argument had been put forward earlier by Adam Smith, but most of the audience would have assumed that he was someone else in the pay of the American Gas Association.

Adam Smith does not, of course, mention the natural gas industry, which did not exist in his time, but he deals with what is the same problem in his discussion of the corn trade. By corn Smith means, of course, wheat. I quote Smith:

> The interest of the inland [corn] dealer, and that of the great body of the people, how opposite soever they may at first sight appear, are, even in the years of the greatest scarcity, exactly the same. It is his interest to raise the price of his corn as high as the real scarcity of the

season requires, and it can never be his interest to raise it higher. By raising the price he discourages the consumption, and puts everybody more or less, but particularly the inferior ranks of people, upon thrift and good management ... If by not raising the price high enough he discourages the consumption so little, that the supply of the season is likely to fall short of the consumption of the season, he not only loses a part of the profit which he might otherwise have made, but he exposes the people to suffer before the end of the season, instead of the hardships of a dearth, the dreadful horrors of a famine.[4]

But, as Smith points out, since the dealer will maximize his profits by adjusting the price at which he sells so that consumption over the season is equal to the supply, he is not likely to put the price too low. Smith adds:

Whoever examines, with attention, the history of the dearths and famines which have affected any part of Europe, during either the course of the present or that of the two preceding centuries, of several of which we have pretty exact accounts, will find, I believe, that a dearth never has arisen from any combination among the inland dealers in corn, nor from any other cause but a real scarcity, occasioned sometimes, perhaps, and in some particular place, by the waste of war, but in by far the greatest number of cases, by the fault of the seasons; and that a famine has never arisen from any other cause but the violence of government attempting, by improper means, to remedy the inconvenience of a dearth ... when the government, in order to remedy the inconveniences of a dearth, orders all the dealers to sell their corn at what it supposes a reasonable price, it either hinders them from bringing it to market, which may sometimes produce a famine even in the beginning of the season; or if they bring it thither, it enables the people, and thereby encourages them to consume it so fast, as must necessarily produce a famine before the end of the season. The unlimited, unrestrained freedom of the corn trade, as it is the only effectual preventative of the miseries of a famine, so it is the best palliative of the inconveniences of a dearth; for the inconveniences of a real scarcity cannot be remedied; they can only be palliated.[5]

Of course, the beneficial role of the merchant in palliating the inconvenience of the scarcity is not understood. 'In years of scarcity the inferior ranks of people impute their distress to the avarice of the corn merchant, who becomes the object of their hatred and indignation'.[6] And Smith points out that this hostility to the merchant shows itself in the laws against 'engrossing and forestalling,' that is, the buying and holding of an inventory to sell at a higher price. Of course, Smith is able to show that the merchant will find his holding of stock profitable only when it is desirable that he should do so. And Smith comments: 'The popular fear of engrossing and forestalling may be compared to the popular terrors and suspicions of witchcraft'.[7] Smith here attempts to discredit the idea that businessmen, by holding stocks, make prices higher than they would otherwise be, by likening it to a belief in witchcraft. Such an analogy would be less effective today – we also believe in witchcraft.

In the two hundred years which have passed since Adam Smith wrote, many economists have argued along much the same lines about the futility of a policy of holding prices below the competitive level. One of these was Edwin Cannan, of the London School of Economics, who wrote in 1915. He was, of course, writing about the price controls established in Britain at the beginning of World War I. He describes the public response to a raise in price:

> Buyers who have to pay higher prices suddenly become either 'the poor' forced to reduce their consumption of necessary articles or else employers of a particularly needy and deserving class which will be thrown out of work by the rise. All the injured persons are at once

represented as being iniquitously robbed by an unscrupulous gang of speculators, middlemen, bloodsucking capitalists, or rack-renting land-lords against whom all the resources of the State ought to be brought forthwith. The ideal somewhat vaguely held seems to be an immediate return to the prices of a few months or a year ago.[8]

Of course, Cannan argues against price controls in the usual way. But he points to a paradoxical aspect of the situation: 'when the price of a thing goes up, [people] abuse, not the buyers nor the persons who might produce it and do not do so, but the persons who are producing and selling it, and thereby keeping down its price'.[9] So, if there is a 'shortage' of wheat or beef or oil, we abuse those who are producing all the wheat, beef, or oil that we have and without whose efforts the 'shortage' would have been still greater. The reason why people show this hostility is that, as Cannan points out, if there is an unusual rise in prices, people

are perfectly convinced that the rise with which they have to contend for the moment is unnatural, artificial, and wholly unjustifiable, being merely the wicked work of people who want to enrich themselves, and who are given the power to do so not by the economic conditions ... but apparently by some absolutely direct and inexplicable interference of the Devil. This has been so since the dawn of history ... but no amount of historical retrospect seems to be of much use. The same absurdity crops up generation after generation.[10]

I began this chapter by saying the economists in their discussion of public policy often deal with questions which are difficult to analyze, about which we know very little, and on which, therefore, our recommendations, if followed, would very likely make things worse. On the other hand, the advice we do have to offer which would be valuable, if followed, consists of a few simple truths.

However, history indicates that these are simple truths which people find it easy to reject – or ignore. When I first began thinking about what I would say, I did not anticipate the present oil problem (and I was not alone). But the character of the public discussion of this problem suggests that we are no better than those who went before us. We are a generation whose time has come. We observe the same attitudes that Cannan described, 'the rise [of price] with which we have to contend at the moment' being 'unnatural, artificial, and wholly unjustifiable … the wicked work of the people who want to enrich themselves'. This raises the question of what the role of an economist should be in a world which rejects the only solidly based advice that he has to give.

Frank Knight, in his presidential address to the American Economic Association in 1950, poses this question – and gives an appropriately depressing answer.

> I have been increasingly moved to wonder whether my job is a job or a racket, whether economists, and particularly economic theorists, may not be in a position that Cicero, concerning Cato, ascribed to the augurs of Rome – that they should cover their faces or burst into laughter when they met on the street … The free-traders, as has been said, win the debates but the protectionists win the elections; and it makes little difference in our policy which party wins, the avowed protectionists or the professed free-traders. Inflation is of course to be brought on as a more pleasant alternative to taxation and then suppressed by law and police action … The serious fact is that the bulk of the really important things that economics has to teach are things that people would see for themselves if they were willing to see. And it is hard to believe in the utility of trying to teach what men refuse to learn or even seriously listen to … Can there be any use in explaining, if it is needful to explain, that fixing a price below the free-market level will create a shortage and one above it a surplus? But the public oh's and ah's and yips and yaps

at the shortage of residential housing and surpluses of eggs and potatoes as if these things presented problems – any more than getting one's footgear soiled by deliberately walking in the mud.[11]

Knight says that, in consequence of this, his interest has tended to shift away from economic theory 'to the question of why people so generally, and the learned elite in particular, as they express themselves in various ways choose nonsense instead of sense,'[12] which is one possible response to the situation, although not, I think, the only one open to us. Knight also says something else which is, I think, helpful to those of us who are looking for an alternative response: 'Explanations of policy might conceivably get farther if we ... ask *why* men believe and practice nonsense but in general act so much less irrationally than they argue – and what follows from that.'[13]

If we took seriously the argument used by those who advocate price controls and similar measures, we would expect much more extreme, and less sensible, proposals than are actually put forward. Thus, some senators believe that lower prices for gasoline would benefit consumers, so they introduce a measure in Congress which would make the gasoline prices of last December [1973] mandatory, not the still lower prices that prevailed in the 1930s. The Federal Power Commission undertook in 1961 to regulate the field price of natural gas – so the level of prices which it determined should be charged in future was that prevailing in 1959–60. As Cannan said, writing long ago and about a different country: 'The ideal somewhat vaguely held seems to be a return to the prices of a few months or a year ago.' Similarly, politicians may make speeches which favor the elimination of all pollution; their proposals are much more moderate. Furthermore, I seem to observe that as the harm inflicted by the policy increases, the strength of the support for that policy decreases – which leads, if not to the elimination of the policy, at any rate to a moderation of it. The Federal Power Commission finally did act to raise the field price of natural gas, although it no doubt acted more slowly and made a smaller change than most economists would have liked. With a rise in the price of oil, concern about the fate of the caribou in Alaska became less pressing, and the Alaska Pipe Line is now likely to be built.

Although controls, such as price and wage controls, are introduced to prevent the basic economic forces from working, a study of the history of controls would show, I believe, that, over a longer period, there have been very few controls which have not been modified to take such forces into account, or even abandoned, so that market forces have free sway. My conclusion is that, although a policy may be misguided, we should not assume that its range, severity, and duration are not kept in check by recognition of the extent of the harm it produces. I do not myself understand why the political system operates in the way it does. Whether the interests opposed to the policy tend to become relatively stronger in the political arena as the amount of harm inflicted by the policy increases or whether recognition of the amount of harm plays a more direct role in the political process, or whether both of these factors operate, I do not know, although it would be my judgment that both of these factors exert some weight. At any rate, it may be that there is room for economists' views on public policy to play a valuable part in this process of modification and change, even though they will usually not be able to exercise a decisive influence over the choice of the policy itself. Certainly, however ill-advised policies may be, they are not in their administration devoid of sense. The demand for nonsense seems to be subject to the universal law of demand: we demand less of it when the price is higher.

A more optimistic view of the role of the economist in the formulation of public policy or, at any rate, of his future role, is presented by George Stigler in his presidential address to the American Economic Association in 1964 entitled, 'The Economist and the State.'[14] Stigler argues that economists in the past have been willing to express views on the role of the state in economic affairs without making any serious study of how the state did in fact carry out the tasks entrusted to it or making any systematic investigation of the comparative performance of state and private enterprise. This was true both for those, like Smith and Alfred Marshall, who wanted to limit government intervention in the economic system and for those, like W. Stanley Jevons, A. C. Pigou, and a host of others, who were in favor of an expanding governmental role. Stigler's comments on our predecessors seem a little harsh – they faced difficulties which we do not encounter, they were few in number, and they were mainly engaged (particularly the better among them) in developing the analysis of a pricing system – but I do not wish particularly to quarrel with his main conclusion. I have argued that our knowledge is very limited, and we are able to read what our predecessors wrote.

Stigler ascribes the lack of influence of economists on the formulation of public policy – which he asserts and I would not wish to deny – to their ignorance. 'Lacking real expertise, and lacking also evangelical ardor, the economist has had little influence upon the evolution of economic policy.'[15] But that is the past. The future, according to Stigler, will be very different.

The age of quantification is now full upon us. We are armed with a bulging arsenal of techniques of quantitative analysis, and of a power – as compared to untrained common sense – comparable to the displacement of archers by cannon ... The desire to measure economic phenomena is now in the ascendent ... It is a scientific revolution of the very first magnitude ... I am convinced the economics is finally at the threshold of its golden age – nay, we already have one foot through the door. The revolution in our thinking has begun to reach public policy, and soon it will make irresistible demands upon us. It will become inconceivable that the margin requirements on securities markets will be altered once a year without knowing whether they have even a modest effect. It will become impossible for an import-quota system to evade the calculus of gains and cost. It will become an occasion for humorous nostalgia when arguments for private and public performance of a given economic activity are conducted by reference to the phrase, external economies, or by recourse to a theorem on perfect competition ... I assert, not that we should make the studies I wish for, but that no-one can delay their coming ... The last half century of economics certifies the immense increase in the power, the care, and the courage of our quantitative researches. Our expanding theoretical and empirical studies will inevitably and irresistibly enter into the subject of public policy, and we shall develop a body of knowledge essential to intelligent policy formulation. And then, quite frankly, I hope that we become the ornaments of democratic society whose opinions on economic policy shall prevail.[16]

I was present when Stigler delivered his address and, as he ended with these words, it was hard to restrain a cheer. When the immediate impact of this eloquent and moving address had passed, Stigler's assertions brought to mind Pope's couplet: 'Hope springs eternal in the human breast;/ Man never is, but always to be, blest.'

But even though we do not believe that such a glittering prospect lies ahead of us, we need not despair. If, as I am inclined to believe, economists cannot usually affect the main course of economic policy, their views may make themselves felt in small ways. An economist who, by his efforts, is able to postpone by a week a government program which wastes $100 million a year (what I consider a modest success) has, by his action, earned his salary for the whole of his life. Indeed, if we compute the total annual salaries of all economists engaged in research on public policy issues (or questions related to this), which might amount to $20 million (or some similar figure), it is clear that this expenditure (or one much larger) would be justified if it led to a minuscule increase in the gross national product. It is not necessary to change the world to justify our salaries. But does the advice of economists on public policy issues improve the situation in those cases in which it does have some influence? I take Stigler's main purpose to be not to raise our morale but to induce us to change our ways so that our advice will be worth following. If, as a result, we achieve my modest aim, we will at least earn our keep. If Stigler's view of the future is correct, we will confer a great benefit on mankind – and be grossly underpaid.

The advice that we have had to offer in the past that was valuable – what I have called the simple truths – was, of course, the implications of a theoretical system which, while its range was restricted, has been confirmed time after time. The assumption of the theory is that producers want to make as much money as possible and that consumers want to get as much for their money as they can. Or, put more generally, and with more applications, it is assumed that people tend, in the main, to pursue their own self-interests. It has proved a very robust theory. But, of course, without knowledge of magnitudes (though they could sometimes be inferred), there were a lot of questions that the theory could not answer. But this hardly explains why the theory has been ignored for those questions for which it could give answers.

Stigler pins his high hopes for the future on the growth in quantitative work. But this development is not without its costs. It absorbs resources which might otherwise be devoted to the development of our theory and to empirical studies of the economic system of a nonquantitative character. Aspects of the economic system which are difficult to measure tend to be neglected. It diverts attention from the economic system itself to the technical problems of measurement. I do not mean to suggest that we should avoid quantitative work. But it is as well to remember that there is no such thing as a free statistic.

I would like to illustrate my view that nonquantative work, or at least work with only the crudest form of quantification, can be of value by means of an example. About 1960 Senator Estes Kefauver was holding hearings into the drug industry and particularly into its practices in introducing new drugs. The main thrust of the hearings was to suggest that the prices paid were too high, but even more that the drugs were often of little or even dubious value. Senator Kefauver concluded that it would be desirable to regulate the introduction of new drugs. At the time this proposal was under consideration the tragic side effects of the use of thalidomide by pregnant women became known. The result was to generate so much support for drug regulation that the Kefauver proposal, which might otherwise have failed to secure congressional approval, was enacted into law in 1962. Was it wise to do this? Consider what one economist said early in 1965 and long before the effects of this new law could be known:

I ask myself a question: Suppose I am a physician in the public health service, and somebody presents to me a new drug. I can approve it now, although we do not know its full effects, and commonly we shall not know the full effects of a new drug for five to ten years after it comes out. If I approve it, and a series of tragedies such as this thalidomide tragedy comes, what will happen to me? I shall certainly be discharged, and I will be held up to public obloquy. The public at large will demand that heads roll. The penalties on me are very heavy indeed if I approve a drug I should not have. Suppose on the other had, that it proves to be a fine drug, and in the long run its achievements are wonderful, but we do not know this yet. If I hold up the use of the drug for five years until all the results are in, a large number of people may die because it was not available. Their survivors will not write and complain that I did not approve the drug earlier. All the penalties are on me in making the mistake of approving the drug too early and none on the mistake of approving it too late. This combination of rewards and penalties ... seems undesirable.[17]

This simple application of the view that people (including government regulators) tend to have regard to their own self-interest leads to the conclusion that the regulation will result in considerable delay in the introduction of new drugs. Those of us who have seen the great improvements in health which have taken place in recent years as a result of the use of newly discovered drugs, particularly in the period since World War II, cannot but feel that the new regulation may have done more harm than good. In this case, it so happens that by now there has been a quantitative study of the effects of the new drug regulation, by Sam Peltzman of the University of California at Los Angeles,[18] and it indicates that apprehension about the legislation was completely justified. The number of new drugs introduced each year on average in the period 1963 to 1970 was about 40 percent of what it had been in the period 1951 to 1962, and a statistical investigation carried out by Peltzman indicates that the whole of this decline was probably due to the new legislation. But he went further. Noting that while some of the drugs excluded from the market by the legislation would have been beneficial, others would no doubt have proved to be unsafe or no better than drugs already existing, Peltzman proceeded to make a calculation of the probable benefits and costs of the new drug regulation. The result: the gains (if any) which accrued from the exclusion of ineffective or harmful drugs were far outweighed by the benefits forgone because effective drugs were not marketed. This conclusion was clearly foreshadowed by the essentially nonquantitative assessment of the probable results of the new drug regulation to which I drew your attention earlier. The economist who made this assessment was Stigler. It represents a fine example of nonquantitative reasoning.

The results obtained by Peltzman were not altogether surprising, since our normal theory would suggest that there would be a decrease (probably large) in the number of new drugs marketed, and, given the benefits which seem to be derived from newly discovered drugs, one would expect that this factor would dominate the results. But what was surprising (and our theory gives us no basis for expecting it) was that there is no strong evidence that the proportion of inefficacious drugs is substantially less

in the smaller number of drugs marketed now than it was
in the years before 1962. All this suggests not that the
decisions of doctors and patients about the use of drugs
are correct but that it is not easy to devise alternative institutions that will perform better.

This is, I believe, a common situation, although economists generally appear to have assumed otherwise. The
reason for this sanguine attitude is that, while most economists do not ignore the inefficiencies of a market system,
which, indeed, they are often prone to exaggerate, they
tend to overlook the inefficiencies inherent in a governmental organization. It is therefore hardly surprising that
economists in the last one hundred years or so have been
led to support (or acquiesce in) an ever-expanding role for
government in economic affairs and have not felt a need
for any serious investigation of the working of governmental organizations. What is wanted, if policy
recommendations are to have a solid foundation, is to take
into account both how a market actually operates and how
a government organization does in fact carry out the tasks
entrusted to it.

Fortunately, the situation I have described does seem
to me in the process of change. Economists (along with
others) are beginning to take a more critical look at the
activities of government, and the kind of study which I
have suggested as desirable is now being made. Certainly
there have been more serious studies made of government regulation of industry in the last fifteen years or so,
particularly in the United States, than in the whole
preceding period. These studies have been both quantitative and nonquantitative. I have referred to studies of
the regulation of natural gas and drugs. But there have
also been studies of the regulation of many diverse activities such as agriculture, aviation, banking, broadcasting,
electricity supply, milk distribution, railroads and trucking, taxicabs, whiskey labeling, and zoning. I mention only
studies with which I am familiar; there are doubtless
many others. The main lesson to be drawn from these
studies is clear: they all tend to suggest that the regula-

tion is either ineffective or that, when it has a noticeable impact, on balance the effect is bad, so that consumers obtain a worse product or a higher-priced product or both as a result of the regulation. Indeed, this result is found so uniformly as to create a puzzle: one would expect to find, in all these studies, at least some government programs that do more good than harm.

In my paper on 'The Problem of Social Cost',[19] I argued that, in choosing between social institutions, the decision should be based on how they would work in practice. I explained that there were costs involved in making market transactions and that consequently there were realloca-tions of factors of production which would, of themselves, raise the value of production but would not take place when the costs of the necessary transactions exceeded the gain in the value of production that would result. Such reallocations of factors can also, of course, be brought about by government regulation. Now government regula-tion also has costs, and government regulators may have in mind ends other than raising the value of production. But the opportunity is there for government regulation to improve on the market. I wrote that 'direct government regulation will not necessarily give better results than leaving the problem to be solved by the market or the firm. But equally there is no reason why, on occasion, such governmental administrative regulation should not lead to an improvement in economic efficiency.'[20]

My puzzle is to explain why these occasions seem to be so rare, if not nonexistent. One explanation would be that these studies happen to have involved cases in which there was a failure of government regulation and that further investigation will uncover many examples of success. But it is hard to feel much confidence in this explanation – the studies have been so numerous and their range so exten-sive, and some of the cases of failure are found where one might have expected success: for example, the control of monopoly, the regulation of drugs or labeling, and zoning. Nonetheless, I am inclined to think that there may be something to this explanation and that, if we looked more at government activities which affected directly the costs of carrying out market transactions, we would indeed find cases in which governmental activities improved the situation. But I would not expect the inclusion of such cases to change the main conclusion, if indeed it is to be regarded as a qualification to it.

Another explanation for this record of poor performance of government would be that this is the way of the world, that the costs of government are always greater than they would be for the market transactions that would accomplish the same result. But I regard this as implausible.

I have come to the conclusion that the most probable reason we obtain these results is that the government is attempting to do too much – that it operates on such a gigantic scale that it has reached the stage at which, for many of its activities, as economists would say, the marginal product is negative. We would expect to reach this stage if the size of an organization were allowed to expand indefinitely. I suspect that this is exactly what has happened. If further studies confirm that this really is the situation, the condition is one which can be cured only by a reduction of government activity in the economic sphere. This will not be easy to achieve, since it runs counter to prevailing attitudes. Oddly enough, the finding that many governmental activities do more harm than good is likely to be received sympathetically. It is common enough to read an article or the account of a speech of which the first part consists of a denunciation of the inefficiency and corruption to be found in the administration of some government program – but this is often followed by a second part which draws our attention to some pressing social problem coupled with the proposal that the government set up a new program or agency or expand an old one to deal with this problem. To ignore the government's poor performance of its present duties when deciding on whether it should or should not take on new duties is obviously wrong (old duties were once, in the main, new duties). But the sanguine view of what the government will accomplish induced by this way of thinking tends to lead to an ever-expanding role for the government in economic affairs (and has done so). If I am right that the attempt to carry out these new activities leads to the government performing worse than before in those that it is already undertaking, the continued expansion of the government's role will inevitably lead us to a situation in which most government activities result in more harm than good. My surmise is that we have reached this stage. This makes an economist's task in one respect easy and in another difficult. It becomes easy because at the present time the advice that has to be given is that all government activities should be curtailed. Our task is made more difficult because our experience with the present overexpanded governmental machine may not give us much indication of what tasks the government should undertake when the sphere of government has been reduced to a more appropriate size. But perhaps I exaggerate the difficulty. The move to a smaller government is hardly likely to be swift – and we will gradually be able to accumulate the information needed to discover what functions should be left to the government.

However, all this assumes that the investigations of economists will, as Stigler claims, in the end have a decisive influence on public policy. Whether the economist will be more successful in limiting the role of government than he has been in policies directly concerned with the operation of the markets and the pricing system remains to be seen. But as I have indicated, even a modest success is not to be despised.

Notes

1. Milton Friedman, 'The Methodology of Positive Economics', in *Essays in Positive Economics* (Chicago: University of Chicago Press, 1953), p. 5.
2. Edmund W. Kitch, 'Regulation of the Field Market for Natural Gas by the Federal Power Commission', *Journal of Law and Economics* (October 1968), p. 243.
3. Edmund W. Kitch, 'The Shortage of Natural Gas', Occasional Paper of the University of Chicago Law School, no. 2 (Chicago, 1971).
4. Adam Smith, *An Inquiry into the Nature and Causes of the Wealth of Nations*, vol. 1 of *The Glasgow Edition of the Works and Correspondence of Adam Smith*, edited by R. H. Campbell and A. S. Skinner (Oxford: Clarendon Press, 1976), p. 524.
5. *Ibid.*, pp. 526–27.
6. *Ibid.*, pp. 527.
7. *Ibid.*, pp. 534.
8. Edwin Cannan, 'Why Some Prices Should Rise', written in 1915 in *An Economists' Protest* (1927), pp. 16–17.
9. *Ibid.*, p. 18.
10. *Ibid.*, p. 23.
11. Frank H. Knight, 'The Role of Principles in Economics and Politics', *American Economic Review* (March 1951), pp. 2–4.
12. *Ibid.*, p. 2.
13. *Ibid.*, p. 4.
14. George J. Stigler, 'The Economist and the State', *American Economic Review* (March 1965), p. 1.
15. *Ibid.*, p. 12.
16. *Ibid.*, pp. 16–17.
17. George J. Stigler, 'The Formation of Economic Policy', in *Current Problems in Political Economy* (Indiana: DePauw University), pp. 74–5.
18. Sam Peltzman, 'An Evaluation of Consumer Protection Legislation: The 1962 Drug Amendments', *Journal of Political Economy* (September–October 1973), p. 1049.
19. R. H. Coase, 'The Problem of Social Cost', *Journal of Law and Economics* (October 1960), pp. 1–44.
20. *Ibid.*, p. 18.

4 On the Decline of Authority of Economists*

William H. Hutt

(1) The 'orthodox' economist is deeply conscious of his impotence to influence opinion

Every independent and serious economist who has some concern for the well-being of the community must, if his beliefs lie in the path of 'orthodox' or Classical tradition, be aware of a periodic recurrence of a sense of utter helplessness. On all sides he thinks he sees the survival of ignorance and confusion of thought on matters which affect human welfare; and he feels that nothing that it is within his power to do or say can have the slightest effect in checking the accumulation of wrong ideas and false policies which they bring forth. He recognizes that in spheres in which policy and action can be influenced, he is doomed to virtual dumbness to-day. He does not attempt the impossible. He seldom protests, for experience and history have taught him that protests are without avail and merely damaging to his reputation. He realizes that persistent opposition to the popular illusions of his time will simply bring him the notoriety of a crank or visionary. He knows that at times, when he happens to be able to support some policy which favors a strong organized interest, his

* The selection is from his *Economists and the Public: A Study of Competition and Opinion*, first published by Jonathan Cape, London, 1936; reprinted by Transaction Publishers, New Brunswick, NJ, 1990. The selection comes from pp. 34–7, 207–17.

pronouncements will be welcomed and he will be acclaimed as an authority. But he does not deceive himself. The same interests that may declare the genius of his one contention will be just as ready to ridicule or quietly ignore his other. His only way to permanent influence is to take a line which will be consistently acceptable to some powerful group or else to pander to the established convictions and conventional beliefs of society at large.

(2) The economist may devote himself to 'pure theory', where he escapes from the sense of frustrated effort

His response may be to retire from that field of intellectual activity in which he could be of direct service to the community and, whilst maintaining verbal contact with the subject matter of economic relations, concentrate on the development of an intricate technique of analysis. He may then find himself the possessor of a logical system which no legislator or administrator could be expected to understand, let alone find of service in the case of any concrete problem. Such an economist will correspond to the 'pure scientist' in other fields. The results of his efforts may occasionally have repercussions of the greatest moment upon knowledge relevant to the sphere of practical affairs (as the techniques of the pure mathematician and the pure physicist have had an immense influence in the field of technology). But his studies can hardly be said to be consciously directed towards that end. He escapes, in consequence, from the sense of baffled striving, of frustrated effort, that confronts his colleague who announces his concern with contemporary happenings. The 'pure theorist' is apt to become a hermit, and whilst he may hope that the practical men may sometimes visit his cave and humbly ask advice on matters in which his mysteries are believed to give him an insight denied to others, in his heart he knows that they have no faith in his mysteries; and they do not genuinely seek his advice; and that if they do come to his lonely dwelling, it is to get from him some mystic formula that happens to suit their purpose, and which can be used with his authority to refute their opponents on some special topic.

(3) It is as a critic of actual affairs that the economist is most aware of his ineffectiveness

On the other hand, the economist's response may be to recognize that his function is, in spite of the public's attitude towards him, to give those who control policy a method which can aid them in their tasks: he may seek to direct his studies into channels in which they may be of service to the ruler and the administrator. Bent on the discovery of a device that will indicate the means of attainment of some specific *economy*, he will consciously ignore many a line of interesting speculation which must inevitably occur to him as he probes into the possibilities offered by the nature of things. It is the economist who interprets his function in this latter way who is most vividly sensitive of his ineffectiveness. He may occasionally seize a favorable opportunity to make just one point in the Press or in a public address. But he knows that even if he gets his message home it will soon be forgotten. In practice, then, he also confines his efforts mainly to writing books and articles that are read only by other economists, and to attempting (if he is a teacher) to disseminate understanding to the successive groups of students who come under his influence. And even here he knows that his powers are small. For not many students among those who are likely to be influential are urged to study economics; and it is only exceptional students who can get very much of a grip of the subject in the three or four years of a first degree course.

(4) Although an expert, no authority attaches to the economist's opinions

It has often been pointed out that the economist in the university is in a different position from most of his scientific colleagues in other branches of study. They are generally believed to be experts in their subject. The man in the street will not usually want to question the teachings of the mathematician, the chemist or biologist. Where the layman does not understand, he will usually take as gospel what the scientist tells him. But whilst there are few intelligent members of the public who would dare to argue with a professor of mathematics about *his* subject, there are few who would *not* be prepared to question the validity of an economist's teachings. Our professional economists would be the last to suggest that the principles they expound are beyond criticism, or that in their suggestions concerning the application of theory they have attained perfect wisdom. Moreover, they must often shudder at the expressed opinions of other teachers whose authority is *believed* to be equal to their own. But the difference in attitude is worth considering. The economist spends as much time in thought and study as his colleagues in the physical or mathematical sciences; and it can hardly be urged that he is less expert in his subject than they are in theirs. Why is it, therefore, that at the present time the views of orthodox economists in the universities are so lightly dismissed by nonacademic controversialists and so seldom sought by legislators? How can the apparent bankruptcy of economic science be explained?

(5) Pre-occupation with refinements of abstract analysis (especially through the mathematical method) may have injured prestige through the repulsion of practical men

The importance of bringing economic thought to bear upon practical affairs has certainly occupied the attention of several economists. Indeed, certain of the leading teachers have been so interested in the question of the *effectiveness* of the science that they appear to have been mainly concerned with the necessity for making known the essentials of economic teaching and with clarifying the central concepts. They have been somewhat impatient of the form taken by some of the attempted refinements of theory, especially of mathematical developments; for they have believed that the result has been to obscure its main lessons and to repel practical-minded 'men of action' from the task of appreciating its meaning. The disinterested student of society must surely recognize an important element of wisdom in this attitude. 'Even the mention of the word "mathematical" makes the average legislator close the book of wisdom altogether,' said [J. Shield] Nicholson in 1913.

(6) Abstract studies have sometimes been accompanied by the loss of that continuous intimacy with reality which should dominate in applied theory, and so have left the student an easy prey to bias

Moreover, the swamping of economic treatises with mathematics has not only tended to drive away the layman, but has diverted attention from fundamentals to points of analytical interest, and incidentally thereby led to some actual corruption or unjustifiable weakening of basic tenets. It cannot be argued, of course, that the mathematical method, building on valid and complete hypotheses, can lead to anything but correct results. Neither can it be contended that this method has not proved, indirectly, of immense value in the development and refinement of the logical framework of the science. But its intricacies appear to have caused some of those practicing it to lose their continuous intimacy with certain broad unquestionable elements of reality which ought always to dominate in applied theory. Whilst not actually inducing generalizations from special cases, some economists seem to have given undue stress to *curiosa* in a manner that has tended to distort their judgment and weaken the authority of economists generally. And they appear frequently to have shown a lack of *judgment* or an unregarded hastiness in framing generalizations from unrealistic premises. Can we wonder at the orthodox *Journal des Economistes*, eager in its desire to secure the embodiment in policy of economic rationalism, showing indifference or even hostility to the new mathematical school which seemed likely to rise on the work of Cournot? For its founder had sought to prove among other things that in some circumstances tariff protection can be an advantage to a national area. And is it surprising that Nicholson should have exclaimed some of the ingenious arguments to justify protective duties: 'These exceptions are simply part of the casuistry of economics; they are like the discussions of moral philosophers of occasional mendacity'?[1] Many strange results are obtainable in the necessarily incomplete studies of abstract theory when particular cases are considered, for so many factors must be presumed to be static that one may be tempted to infer from the apparent chaos that valid generalizations applicable to real society are impossible; and there may be so much indefiniteness in the economist's mind that when attempting to apply his science to practical problems he will be an easy prey to the bias of his sympathies.[2] Some of the dangers have been well demonstrated by Dr J. R. Hicks, who, whilst himself a mathematical economist and a convinced believer in the past and present usefulness of that method, has realized the pitfalls. The *incompleteness* of the speculations of Edgeworth (followed particularly by Marshall) on the indeterminateness of price under isolated bilateral monopoly led to a weakening of the economists' teaching on the subject of labor combinations which *may* have contributed most seriously to gross errors in public policy. The effect has been, says Dr Hicks, to wrap

> the determination of wages under competition in a web of obscurity, by distracting attention from the significant factors in the problem, and concentrating on ultra-theoretical points of which the importance in actual practice is very questionable. What is worse, the mathematical theorists, after raising these special difficulties, have not completely cleared them up.[3]

(7) The valid scope of abstract method has often been misunderstood, and the frankness of the expositors of economic theory has wrongly disparaged the economists' authority[4]

An extremely clear example of the dangers involved in the pre-occupation of some economists with the logic or mathematics of the science is seen in an important contribution to abstract theory by one of the younger economists which seems unconsciously to reflect misconceptions which are common in certain schools of thought. In this case the author, Mrs Joan Robinson, was bold enough in the first and existing edition of her book[5] not only to apologize for the uselessness (to the practical man) of her own contribution, but to belittle in the plainest terms the value of orthodox method in its present state of development as an aid to the guidance of practical policy. She said that the analytical economist is:

> conscious in the presence of the practical man, of an agonizing sense of shame. And when he tries to work on some fresh problem and sets about writing out the assumptions which are necessary to make it soluble, he cannot help imagining what the mocking comment of the practical man would be if his eyes happened to fall on that list of assumptions.[6]

Now these sweeping and possibly light-hearted assertions amount to a libel on those theorists, past or present, who do not happen to subscribe to her views as to the omniscience of the methods she chooses to adopt, or her opinions as to how abstract analysis is serviceable in practical problems. They are assertions against which it might be difficult for those slighted to protest; for they must be only too conscious of the desirability of further exploration along many paths; and self-defense might be interrupted as complacent self-satisfaction. The truth is that what may be regarded as modern orthodox theory throws the clearest light upon countless aspects of the affairs of the actual world. The utilization of that theoretical system does not necessarily involve any disputed or disputable assumptions whatsoever. What is called 'economic theory' can be logically and usefully applied to the great majority of concrete problems which involve the contemplation of *scarce means*. But Mrs Robinson said in effect:

Be patient. It is true that all the economists from the Classical writers onwards have been hopelessly wrong, but that was because their theories were based on the assumption of competition. Now, however, there is hope. We have invented marginal revenue curves and can start from the assumption of monopoly. By means of skillful a priori reasoning based on mathematics and geometry, we shall one day understand things. So in the meantime it behoves us to be careful not to say anything which might reflect upon any existing policy. When we have developed our geometrical theorems to the necessary degree of complexity, we may find ultimately that the universal monopoly is better than any other conceivable state of affairs. So far, some of our studies, based on necessarily absurd assumptions, show that monopoly might sometimes be beneficial. So go ahead with your dynamiting of shipyards and other forms of 'rationalization', with your closing down of paying coal mines, with your burning of coffee, with your ploughing under of wheat and cotton lands, with your pools, and marketing boards, and transport boards, with your compulsory co-operation, tariffs, and import quotas, or wage and price fixation. We have nothing to say for them or against them. But above all, beware of economists who suggest to you that there is a strong presumption that these things are harmful. They are charlatans. They are only guessing. In their hearts they are ashamed of themselves. They are making unjustifiable assumptions which would shock you if you only knew what they were.

This is hardly a misrepresentation of the impression that her Introduction must leave with a casual reader. The tragedy is, however, that the actual charlatans of the economic world are just those writers, usually with considerable popular reputations as economists, who possess the most meager grasp of economic theory. Such persons will have neither the necessary training nor the inclination to read and understand her book, but the introductory chapter will enable them the more easily to cloak their incompetence in claiming sole efficacy for the 'empirical method'.

(8) Refinement of analysis has tended to become an end rather than a means

What Mrs Robinson failed to realize in 1933 was that the limitations of mathematical and other abstract methods in economics will never be removed by mere refinement. The expansion of analysis for its own sake may, of course, prove profitable. The world is deeply indebted to abstract speculation in the social as well as in the physical sciences. To realize the magnitude of that debt in the field of economic theory we have only to consider the all-unconscious yet utter confusion in the mind of so eminent a logician as J. S. Mill when he tackled a fundamental problem in value. The notions of the mathematicians easily resolved the difficulties that so perplexed him; and this was accomplished through the medium of the simplest conceptions.[7] But the social organism cannot be fruitfully studied by classifying facts into categories which will fit into a given scheme of analysis. The student's attention must be devoted to observation, to recognizing the nature of the community and its activities, to appreciating to the full its real complexities and the imponderable elements in it. The nomenclature, conceptions and logical methods ingrained in his mind by habits acquired as a student of theory should guide his efforts, unobtrusively as a rule. When they are relevant, he should have easy recourse to them; they should keep him continuously aware of the extent of his assumptions; but they should never be allowed to dominate his investigations. Brevity and convenience in exposition may often justify his borrowing terms and concepts from abstract science, even when dealing with practical issues; yet, in much of the best work in applied economics, one is not reminded of any specific analytical apparatus having been employed at all. The apparatus of economics, as Cairnes pointed out, is mere 'scaffolding'. 'It must ever be borne in mind', he said, 'that in Political Economy, as in all the positive sciences, classification, definition, nomenclature, *is* scaffolding and *not* foundation – consequently a part of the work which we must always be prepared to modify or cast aside as soon as it is found to interfere with the progress of the building'.[8]

(9) The mistaken notion has been preached that when results of theories based on unreal hypotheses have to be expressed in imaginary terms, economic science has failed

The strictures in Mrs Robinson's book actually apply, not generally, as she believed, but to those analytical theorists alone who have failed to understand both the usefulness and the limitations of their work. They appear to have been misled either by a false conviction that logical method can be usefully applied only to phenomena which can be classified with reference to the convenience of their own favorite analytical machine, or by an illusion that the machine is more important than the task. To force certain practical problems into their system, it has sometimes been necessary to make assumptions which, judged by actual conditions, are certainly absurd. No exception can be taken to this procedure for work in the purely abstract sphere. Simplicity of assumptions makes it possible to erect, by the mathematical method, an intricate logical structure; and, as we have admitted, such a method can be fruitful in many ways. Yet the results reached have often to be expressed in imaginary terms which have virtually no parallel in the world of reality. This does not prove, however, that economic science has failed.[9] It shows that the results of much abstract speculation in the economic as in other fields of inquiry are apparently or actually barren. Because the theorists of the mathematical and diagrammatical schools are in some cases unable to find realistic categories with which their method can satisfactorily deal, that does not prove that other means of so doing do not exist.

(10) Cannan fought for simplicity of exposition in order that it might be shown how society could be made 'better off'

The stalwarts who, during the past generation, fought most strongly in England against the tendency for intricate abstractions to dominate academic economics were Edwin Cannan and J. Shield Nicholson. Cannan's outlook, which was maintained in his subsequent work, was clearly set forth in his Presidential Address to Section F of the British Association in 1902. His case was expressed with admirable simplicity; it is doubtful whether on common-sense grounds it would be questioned at any point by a responsible economist; and it is certain that if the point of view for which he pleaded could have become an effective influence in practical affairs or in the public mind, many of the colossal mistakes of British internal and external policy since that time would have been avoided. Fundamental to his attitude was the necessity for opening the eyes of inquirers and the community generally 'to the wonderful way in which the people of the whole civilized world now cooperate in the production of wealth'.[10] Such an attitude is easily capable of misrepresentation. It is not difficult to suggest that it reflects special pleading for an existing regime. But it does stress a basic aspect of social cooperation which has struck all disinterested and scientific students of society in the modern age, yet which has still no popular recognition. Cannan seems to have been afraid that the public mind would be led away from basic essentials of this nature owing to the diffusion of effort in devoting attention to ingenious futilities in the pedantries of an academic atmosphere. His fears of the new tendencies were vividly expressed in 1904. He pictured the discomfiture of a young man, staggered by the contrast between riches and poverty, when he approaches a professor of economics to learn the causes of such apparent injustice. The professor treats him to a simple diagrammatic exposition of distribution and carefully explains each step. But the would-be student still finds the real problems that were worrying him unanswered. 'He wanted bread, and the professor has given him a stone.'[11] Nearly thirty years later Cannan had clung resolutely to his original view. Criticizing the plea of Professor Robbins for the desirability of regarding economics as a study of 'human behavior as a relationship between ends and scarce means which have alternative uses', and for the elimination of the concept of social utility and the notion of material welfare as the economic criteria, Cannan said:

> Mankind has modified (the economic system) from time to time through the ages with the intention of making it – this gigantic machine – do its work better, and there has been very little doubt about the meaning of doing it better. When people ask the professor whether such and such a change will be good or bad, they will only find him tiresome if he pretends that he knows nothing of good and bad ends in economic matters and can only talk about the cheapness or dearness of different ways of attaining a given end. They will say: 'You know perfectly well that what we want from you is to be told whether this proposed change will make us and our children better off ...' Benefactors endow Chairs of Economics, audiences listen to economic lectures, purchasers buy economic books, because they think that understanding economics will make people better off. Is it really necessary for professors of economics to destroy this demand for economic teaching by alleging that they do not know what 'better off' means?[12]

The importance of this passage lies, not in its criticism of Professor Robbins's view of the scope of economic science, but in its insistence that there are certain radical truths connected with the process of 'making people better off', the consideration of which should be central to all serious economic study; and recent tendencies, it is feared, have been diverting attention from the essential realities with which economic theory should be ultimately concerned. Cannan's concern was with the *prestige* of economic science, for it is on this that its practical influence must be built. Our own suggestion is that whilst the impressive developments in the logical structure of Political Economy which the last forty years have witnessed are valuable contributions to the physiology of economic method, they have tended, in their treatment by some of the most fertile methodological inventors, seriously to obscure the persistent relevance of the backbone of the science, and to confuse the realism of its approach.

(11) Nicholson similarly deplored developments which 'did not lend themselves to popular representation'

Nicholson took a more extreme but very similar line to Cannan. He was inclined to go back as far as J. S. Mill in tracing the evil influence of undue abstraction! He blamed him for having built on Ricardo's theories instead of trying, in his *Principles*, to bring the common sense of Adam Smith down to date. Nicholson seemed to find this fact the origin of the unjustified revolt which Mill himself led against his own doctrine. In recent times, he thought, attempted refinements of doctrine had led to the

> domination of certain economic ideas and methods which do not lend themselves to popular representation ... When they are applied to 'political economy considered as a branch of the science of a statesman or legislator' (Adam Smith), or to the 'art of political economy' (Sidgwick), they fall for the most part into the wide realm of inappropriate conceptions'.[13]

And he quoted with approval Sir Llewellyn Smith's contention that 'on all grounds it would be deplorable if through the obscurity of its language economic science should relapse into the position of an esoteric doctrine confined to a small circle of initiates, only the bare results of which are capable of dogmatic statement to the whole outside world'.[14]

(12) Although Professor Robbins has argued that 'it is no service to knowledge to make things simpler than they are', it is obvious that popular expositions have not injured authority in other sciences

It is a remarkable but significant thing that Professor Robbins, who has studied in the Cannan tradition, should have come to what at first appears to be an almost opposite outlook. He has expressed the belief that:

> the hope that Economics will ever become something which the layman can comprehend without training is doomed for ever to frustration ... the world of economic reality is a complicated thing, and it is not to be expected that as we come to understand it better our generalizations should be less complicated. It is no service to knowledge to make things simpler than they are. And indeed I am inclined to think that if we as economists devote ourselves too much to attempts at popularization, we shall be doing our science a disservice, and limiting its chances of beneficial influence. The sort of Economics which the Press and the public would like is an Economics which is bound either to be wrong or to be misapprehended. Surely it is better to push ahead with our analysis, embrace technicality with open arms if technicality will help us, and come to be so frequently right that we acquire the respect now given without question to the practitioners of the natural sciences.[15]

This controversy, if that is the right word, seems to be largely beside the point. The physical sciences have not been injured by popular science writings. It is true that however simply the arguments of modern economics are expressed, they will remain abstractions, and so peculiarly liable both to misapprehension and misinterpretation no matter how clear or concrete the illustrations. Even Adam Smith was told by Burke: 'You, Dr. Smith, from your professor's chair, may send forth theories upon freedom of commerce as if you were lecturing on pure mathematics; but legislators must proceed by slow degrees.' Misunderstanding and misrepresentation are inevitable. Yet it is of the greatest importance in any democratic State that some persons at any rate shall persevere and experiment in the task of popularizing economic truths.

Notes

1. Quoted in Palgrave's *Dictionary*, article on 'Production'.
2. Our references to Jevons in Chapter X are relevant here, for he was a leading pioneer in the development of the mathematical method. The coldness of abstract conceptions and symbols is no certain safeguard against bias.
3. Errors of the same kind have arisen in connection with the mathematical economists' discussion of discrimination. See Hutt, 'Discriminating Monopoly and the Consumer', *Economic Journal*, March 1936. The complexities of contemporary discussions of decreasing costs give rise to similar dangers. See also *Economic Journal* (1930), p. 215.
4. Much of this and the following three paragraphs appeared in Hutt, 'Economic Method and the Concept of Competition', *South African Journal of Economics*, March 1934.
5. *Economics of Imperfect Competition.* We refer to her views in the past tense as we do not believe she will adhere to them.
6. *Op. cit.*, p. 2.
7. Mill summarized his difficulties as follows: 'The demand, therefore, partly depends on the value. But it was before laid down that the value depends on the demand. From this contradiction how shall we extricate ourselves? How solve the paradox, of two things, each depending upon the other?' (*Principles*, Ashley Edition, p. 446). The English economists were slow to perceive the relevance of mathematical method. Cairnes doubted in 1875 whether 'economic truths' were 'discoverable through the instrumentality of mathematics' and said that he was unaware of any case of this. (*Character and Logical Method of Political Economy*, 2nd edn, preface, p. iv.)
8. Cairnes, *op. cit.*, p. 146.
9. There is, nevertheless, a real danger in such methods in that

illustrations may be uncritically sought from actual affairs. For instance, Mrs Robinson, after having demonstrated that under certain hypothetical cost and price schedules, a fall in demand would result in a rational monopolist raising his prices, and that under other schedules a rise in demand would be met by a decrease of output, appeared to assume that she had provided an explanation of these very common phenomena of the industrial world (pp. 72 and 66). But a close study of actual cases would show that the true causes are as far removed from the circumstances she postulated as they are from the typical explanations of the industrialists themselves.

10.   Cannan, *The Economic Outlook*, p. 174.
11.   *Ibid.*, p. 221.
12.   *Economic Journal*, 1932, pp. 425–6.
13.   *Quarterly Review*, 1913, p. 409.
14.   Quoted *ibid.*, p. 412.
15.   *Economica*, 1930, pp. 23–4. Professor Robbins's practice has hardly conformed to these precepts! His *Great Depression* is a brilliant piece of popularization.

5 'Realism' in Policy Espousal*

Clarence Philbrook[1]

Economists in general have learned to live under the recurring charge that they are 'unrealistic'. The term may, of course, mean many things. Where the meaning applies to what they do strictly as 'scientists,' the barbs need not go deep. Against such slings and arrows there hangs ready a familiar armor – namely, the prestige of scientific method, made magically tough by having clothed also those heroes of the battle for knowledge, the natural scientists. Not always are economists content, however, to remain 'scientists' describing relationships and eschewing reference to the desirability of things, or even to remain 'engineers' suggesting devices to achieve ends laid before them entirely by others. They do step out of these rôles and give their society, or some sector of it, advice which commits the adviser to responsibility for value judgments.[2] They do 'take positions' and act as advisers in a full sense. In this rôle too they are often faced with the charge of being 'unrealistic'.

Used in this connection the epithet becomes a different missile and will not be turned aside by the same armor. What range of meanings may possibly attach to the term need not for present purposes be explored. One particular connotation which it frequently carries will be singled out and attributed to the word. This meaning is, that the economist charged with 'unrealism' has made recommendations requiring for their fulfillment changes in things which must, for the purpose at hand, be treated

---

* From *American Economic Review*, Vol. 43 (December 1953), pp. 846–59.

as unchangeable. It would be brash to deny that such a charge may often be true. A basic responsibility implied in it has, at any rate, a valid claim to attention: *of course* the economist, to give useful advice to society, must regard various things as in a significant sense beyond our power to alter. Failure to do this seems virtually a definition of idle dreaming. Wherever he has failed to be guided properly by this precept, the economist must indeed confess that he has sinned.

Yet there is a more cankerous sin which economists have all too often committed in order to escape indictment. So great has become the scramble to turn state's evidence, that one who suggests a solution not treating as 'given' ('here to stay') any particular popular social practice is merely fortunate if no colleague misquotes him Carlyle's response to Margaret Fuller's decision to accept the reality of the universe: 'Egad, you'd better!' The charge of 'unrealism' is used with telling effect to discredit policy recommendations without adequate consideration. It probably affects in no small degree the determination of what types of work are respected and supported in universities. Science has rightly been said to aim at stability of belief by cultivating doubt; but the spirit behind the familiar charge, by restricting the range of questioning deemed worth while, limits the use of science for this fundamental purpose. In so doing that spirit, on the negative side, creates a presumption that the time of scholars is readily available for other activity, and, on the positive side, implies that worthy uses for time must be sought elsewhere. It therefore fosters a test of scholars which, at a moderate stage of development, asks whether their activity is 'constructive'. (Does it build, not tear down? Does it look forward, not backward?) And, at a now common extreme, asks whether their activity immediately and discernibly influences practical affairs. Of course the man least demonstrably ineffectual is he who advises others to do what he knows they will do without his advice. Indeed, the competition for reputation as 'realists' works toward a condition in which students of society are loath to take a minority position. Society tends as a result to lose the benefit of that disinterested, fundamental, continuous criticism which, unless provided by persons made independent of practical affairs for that very purpose, is unlikely to be forthcoming. There has grown a widespread practice of cooperation with 'things as they are,' without explicit criticism of them, which is bound to have the effect of active approval regardless of whether such is intended. Thus the spirit of 'Egad, you'd better!' bids fair to render the field of political economy not merely useless but actually damaging to the social welfare.

However, I wish to invite contemplation and discussion; for the practical consequences hinging upon the treatment of this issue are enormous, and yet the matter seldom crosses the threshold into systematic consensus-seeking, but rather remains a little-explored source of recurring irritation and *ad hoc* dicta. I should like, therefore, to avoid resting upon the controversial conclusion stated above, and find a more neutral point of departure.

Perhaps this can be found along the following lines. In deciding what advice to give, one clearly must regard some conditions as given. On the other hand, the very fact that someone is to be advised to do something which presumably he might not otherwise do means that not everything in the situation is being treated as given. Evidently what is at issue is 'correctness' in the selection of things to be so treated. If we can find literally no criteria, consensus on policy is indeed hard to come by. It must then be impossible to force the 'unrealist' to regard the necessary things as fixed; and, on the other hand, his critic can always, by 'realistically' accepting the universe of his choice, find sanctuary against the necessity of defending his own positive policies. Is it possible to say anything helpful toward consensus about what actually constitutes 'realism,' in some defensible sense, in the selection of proposals on policy? It may turn out so, if we explore a path through a series of intellectual positions, asking how far it may reasonably be supposed that plaintiff and defendant can walk together and where they might feel forced to part company. The method will be to start with a position which a 'realist' surely will not think labels alterable any conditions which are not so, and progressively introduce elements which he might consider less 'realistic,' at each stage inquiring whether he really would be likely to reject the new element. Finally the question will be raised whether the 'realist' can reasonably insist upon any principle which would enable him to use meaningfully the familiar charge. An effort will be made to maximize the ease with which any telling rebuttal that may be available against the argument of this chapter can be made, so that if the conclusions reached here are wrong the fact may be made clear and many of us may mend our ways in keeping with a sound 'realism'.

The position most safely 'realistic' would seem to be that which took *everything* in the situation as given, including both the physical universe and the attitudes of all persons. One who adopted it would presumably interest himself exclusively in the discovery of regularities and the forecasting of events. The fact that this view by no means corresponds to the scientific outlook in total does not assure that the two are never thought to be identical. Such identification probably accounts in no small measure for the high prestige of simply any 'empirical' research as opposed to 'arm-chair theorizing': almost any conceivable collection of figures will be regarded in important quarters as representing a certain hard-headed practicality, while any serious discussion of what is the real significance of the collection is considered either jealous carping or mere mental gymnastics by minds too lazy to do 'constructive' work. Finding 'what the facts are' is the great task according to this view; for, if they were once discovered, we should then be in position to make forecasts.

This position has great appeal to men of scientific bent, and indeed to all of us. It is 'obvious' to common sense that every effect must have a cause and that any state of mind must be an effect of preceding states of mind, body, and environment. To be sure, some embarrassment may arise in trying to find a function and purpose for the scientist himself; for, although the surrounding stimuli may cause him to emit sounds and cause us to call the sounds a forecast, he cannot in this view 'influence' anything, and the notion of function, including that of purpose, is itself meaningless. Nevertheless, the mere fact that an analyst will typically use words which imply that his conclusions are yet to be determined by the effort of investigation or discussion does not prove the deterministic position false. Activity that is apparently purposeful may be viewed either as the result of a free will operating with its available means toward some goal, or alternatively, as the movement of a set of pre-established forces working toward equilibrium. In the determinist view the pseudo function of the scientist is that of a cog in a machine. The tempting query why, if determinism is true, the scientist would struggle as he does, or society pay him to do so, is itself meaningless, for 'would' no longer can connote volition and 'struggle' has no meaning; he and society do not do, in any significant sense, what they think best – they simply do.

The well-known and fatal difficulty with the deterministic attitude that we must treat everything as given is that the truth of its opposite also is obvious and is inevitably dominant in our procedure. It is certainly impossible for the mind to act regularly as if it regarded itself as an epiphenomenon accompanying the burning out of a physiochemical reaction. Although nuclear physicists could not alter the fact of the fission ability of the atom, it is said that some of them believe they could (as well as should) have refused to discover the fact or, at least, to put it to its most famous use. No analyst will, where it counts, cling to a purely deterministic position. All will 'play like' their 'decisions' are decisions in the common-sense meaning of the word and capable of affecting reality.

Social analysts as advisers will, then, take one step away from regarding everything as given and still feel themselves to be 'realists'. The most modest step is exemplified where the analyst occupies an administrative post with some discretionary power. A man in that position would believe that the word 'discretion' had some meaning – that the external situation could be influenced by a *decision*, such as, for example, to allow a certain wage rate to be raised. The step is modest in that it leaves the scientist in the same instrumentalistic relation to the situation as he might bear to a group of chemical materials to be manipulated. Further, nearly all social analysts would take another step without at all losing a sense of 'realism,' in believing that they might actually influence the world by giving advice to critically placed administrators or legislators – on occasion simply by making evident to them the truth of a cause-and-effect sequence or the validity of a value. Indeed, adding together these two steps, we have the basis for what appears to be regarded as the most valuable activity of analysts as social advisers, although a relatively high respectability seems to attach also to the act of advising organized pressure groups.

The range of possible change, and of influence of the social adviser, is relatively narrow if channels of influence are restricted to those just mentioned. For most important changes (usually legal) require a change of attitudes on the part of a large number of persons. This need not appear true, to be sure, to one willing to take a purely instrumentalistic view. In that outlook, the range of action would be considerably broader, since it would be possible to advise holders of power to use their power 'for the good of the people' with small regard for what the people thought they wanted. Indeed, much recent history of government might be accounted for in terms of a general belief that 'realism' is violated by those who hope social advisers may have influence otherwise than directly. This instrumentalistic position need not disavow the possibility of change in mass attitudes: a benevolent government may 'educate' the people to agreement with its measures. This is a clear-cut, possible intellectual outlook; but if such neo-Machiavellianism is to be espoused, the social scientists adopting it should make as clear as they can that they have given up hope of that consensus-created,   not   merely   consensus-creating, government which is usually called democracy. Those who believe that consensus should precede political action must, it is merely tautological to say, believe the archetype of their 'action' as advisers to consist of effort to help others discover correct attitudes; so we may suppose that, in considering attitudes to be among the alterable conditions, we still have the company of 'realists' whose ultimate values include a rôle for democracy.

Since important changes in society do require alterations in the attitudes of many persons, social analysts, in order to form opinions on what changes would be worth while if they could be brought about, must often consider at great length what processes would go forward under assumed conditions which are often at variance with the facts. Strangely, by carrying on such considerations carefully rather than carelessly, men call down upon their heads some of the most scornful charges: 'unrealistic,' 'too theoretical,' 'purist,' and so on. Yet it is difficult to see what could be more 'unrealistic' than saying that a change would be worth while (unless mere change for its own sake is the sole issue) without first methodically considering what results might reasonably be expected. So surely it may be assumed that the school of 'realism' would accept the study of 'models,' or 'theories,' as indispensable.

It is in deciding what alterations of attitude to attempt, that the point arises which presumably most persons stressing 'realism' have in mind. Should we not, they might ask, distinguish among conceivable changes according to whether we stand some reasonable chance of actually effecting the necessary shift of attitude? Why waste effort by making suggestions which we cannot hope will be accepted? These queries appear to have much justice. The idea obviously is that one ought to list the actions open to him and attach to each a weight determined by the probability that it would in fact bring about the attitude change intended.

If we described a 'pure realist' position as calling for decision by simply selecting the advice with the highest 'probability' weight, we ought to be able to treat it as only a straw man. To be sure, the mere fact that most 'realists' would reject an approach so stated does not mean it really differs from what they have effectively in mind; a major part of the thesis of this chapter is that numerous economists are in effect espousing positions which, if stated clearly, would be repudiated by them. Nevertheless, one fatal criticism of any such bald 'probability' approach must surely be treated as noncontroversial. No one would explicitly maintain that a high relative probability of having *some* effect should give priority to an act completely without regard to the relative desirability of the outcome it would tend to have. It seems reasonable to suppose, therefore, that the 'realist' would accept as a part of 'realism' the necessity of consulting end values as determinants of advice.

It becomes important, then, to recall what is required in due allowance for this element of 'realism'; for, although few would deny its claims in the abstract, many become quite impatient when called upon in specific cases to give full weight to it. (Who having experienced the earlier years of the New Deal can forget how frequently the conclusive defense of almost any policy was that the government was *doing something*!)

Evidently the adviser, having arrayed the lines of advice he might give on a particular issue, must assign a weight to each according to the desirability of the change it would tend to promote. A change can be desirable otherwise than for the sake of novelty only as it furthers some end. But since there are conflicts of ends, an action may further one end and lessen the realization of another, and the net significance cannot be known without first evaluating the various ends (or degrees of realization of them). Relative evaluation requires a common measure, hence can be accomplished only if the 'ends' are but intermediate, serving in turn as means to, and deriving their value from, a more general end (which itself is merely one of a number of ends all serving as means to a yet more nearly ultimate goal). Assigning the correct desirability weight to a change means judging its net influence upon the realization of some end sufficiently general ('high') to include the intermediate ends touched by the change; and this judgment involves tracing the effects of the change upon each intermediate end and evaluating those effects in each case by reference to the inclusive end. Thus, literally full justification of the whole set of value weights one attaches to a set of policy suggestions would require laying bare the relations between the proposed changes and some all-subsuming, ultimate end of social organization. Only in this way could the mutual consistency of all the various means and subsidiary ends which constitute a total program for society be established.

In discussion aimed at consensus, the problem is one of showing a disputed policy to be a means to some intermediate end and then inquiring, of parties to the discussion, whether this 'end' is in their view necessary as a means to what they regard as some more fundamental goal. If not, agreement is not logically called for. The proponent must then try to show that the disputed 'end' is a means to something he himself regards a more fundamental end, and if successful repeat the query. It is for present purposes unnecessary to dwell upon the complexities hidden under the light reference to showing a disputed end to be a means; what is needed is merely a suggestion of the extensiveness of the obligation taken on by acceptance of the necessity of value weights and consensus. If consensus is to be soundly reached, a process of the sort indicated must go forward until the derivation of importance is traced back to some end the authenticity of which is accepted by the parties to the discussion. Fortunately, it is usually not necessary to go far toward ultimates; but the ideal student of policy, far from refusing to talk about the sheer desirability of a proposal opposed to his own, would stand ready and eager to reduce the two, no matter how different, to commensurability in the manner suggested.

There is good reason to be appalled by the difficulty of the task cited, especially in a world become self-conscious and discordant about its values. It is of no avail, however, to assail as 'purists,' 'absolutists,' or 'unrealists' those who call attention to the task. The only alternative to readiness to defend a position in the sense indicated is to grant that at least some of one's means and intermediate ends have not been tested for mutual consistency, and that one's policy proposals have therefore no more authority than some diametrically opposite set. These considerations surely place a demand upon an economist giving advice on social policy that he shall have thought his way through, so far as the state of knowledge makes possible, to an internally consistent model of economic organization on which he bases his advice. The gravity of the potential effect of error in policy, and the immensity of the scope for growth and ripening of intellect toward power to grapple with the problems involved in discerning good policy, render merely ludicrous the widespread impatience toward 'armchair theorizing,' which, unless the integrity of the men involved is in question, must be regarded as an arduous process of critical contemplation and integration aimed at the development of wisdom.

Of course nothing in the foregoing discussion denies the notion that the end must be dealt with in the light of the availability of means. Neither is it affirmed that 'the end justifies the means' in the sense that there is any end for the furtherance of which no device is too bad; but the ultimate end itself must contain criteria of acceptability of means, so that the means, if justified, are indeed justified by the end. Even though strong doses of starvation might have shortened immensely the employment depression of the 1930s, the ends of the society justified the relief of distress. These things are probably all that need saying about the perennial argument over the short-run versus the long-run view in the selection of policy; yet one's faith that the full import of attributing value weights is noncontroversial is bound to be shaken by memory of how often any manifestation of the long-run view is answered with some form of the completely irrelevant 'realistic' proposition, 'In the long run we are all dead.' Although this reaction has done much damage to the search for sound policy, by limiting the consideration of ends, it may nevertheless reasonably be interpreted as something other than repudiation (in the abstract) of thinking in terms of ends and means. Indeed, it is probably as a rule a confused, distorted, and misapplied criticism, not of means-ends thinking but of presumed failure to apply fully such a calculus. More often than not, the thought reflected is simply a generalization of the example given above: the idea that the time dimension must be allowed for – that radical change takes time and meanwhile we must make the best of the situation, perhaps by means which hamper realization of some accepted goal. To be sure, a proposal involving thought of the long run might often be criticized because it seemed to violate the true 'probability' approach, which we shall in a moment try to state. But it may be taken for granted, relatively few 'realists' would question that in such an approach value considerations must have a place.

It seems possible now to sum up the most likely meaning of a 'probability' approach – a position which must be the one that would be held by any who, in the light of considerable discussion, still were willing to make use of the charge, 'unrealistic'. Although in some cases only under pressure, they surely would accept these propositions: that many elements in a social situation are capable of change, including the attitudes which determine policy; that actions of individuals in their rôle of 'social advisers' could have some influence on those attitudes; and that the advice to be given by them cannot be chosen without the aid of weights attached to different lines of advice according to the relative desirability of the change which these respectively would tend to further. They would insist, however, that a choice can be made only after superimposing another weight on each line of advice according to the probability of its taking effect if offered. Men called 'unrealistic' are those who disregard this principle and presumably those who assign probability weights incorrectly.

There is a considerable appearance of reason about this method of thought. Still, it requires the most careful inspection.

It is important not to slight the fact that two lines of advice such as typically give rise to controversy over 'realism' are not necessarily so related as to make 'probability' considerations relevant at all. A believer in states' rights, for example, presumably may make clear his belief while yet offering good counsel on how best to operate a program which disregards such a conception. The relation required if 'probability' is to have any place is that the two lines of advice be truly alternative: that is, mutually exclusive.

Two possible causes of mutual exclusiveness are suggested. First, sheer limitation on time, energy, and intellect requires specialization; and some decision must be made as to the field in which to develop special competence. May one not make an ample contribution by advising the Federal Reserve authorities how best to use their powers, without questioning whether the present banking system is the best conceivable? Actually, specialization raises no problem. The question is whether, not having studied the possibilities of alternative systems, the specialist causes or allows it to be supposed that his activities constitute support of this system against alternatives or whether, having decided another system would be better, he conceals the fact. If one applies 'probability' thinking and recommends that approach for others, it must be from sources other than specialization that he derives the implied mutual exclusiveness of different pieces of advice.

The second cause of mutual exclusiveness which the 'realist' presumably has in mind is that the very act of approving a different general course may destroy power to guide action along the best path in an established, although less desirable, direction. There is no denying that suggestions from one listed among the faithful with respect to a program are, as 'self-criticism,' more likely to wield influence than is advice from 'outsiders'. Thus we can identify conceptually a type of case in which the lines of advice are alternative in a sense sufficient to justify at least entertaining the question of whether it is desirable to be guided by 'probability'.

It goes without saying that the mere identification of such a class of cases gives no license to beg the question of whether any particular case belongs to the class. If indeed 'probabilities' are sometimes a proper guide, the epithet 'unrealistic' can at best be justified only upon an explicit showing that giving one of the lines of advice does preclude the usefulness of giving the other. But even for use in cases where 'probability' is formally relevant the 'probability' approach is open to grave doubt on a number of scores.

In the first place, what is the criterion for the relative weighting of a 'degree of probability' and a 'degree of desirability'? There is always the devastating possibility that the total weight of an action in keeping with a completely evil outcome might be greater than that of one tending to further a desirable end. Suppose that in Germany under Hitler it appeared that one hundred thousand Jews would probably be bayoneted to death. Should I, if a German, have suggested merely a less brutal execution by gas – thus quite possibly doing *some* good – or should I have cried out against the whole idea, quite probably having no discernible influence? And, if I decided on the former, should I have claimed credit as a 'realist' and decried as 'unrealistic' any who advised the society to let the Jews live?

In the second place, the problem of actually assigning 'probabilities' must be faced, some aspects of which are relegated to our third and fourth points. At present we may consider the matter from a relatively uncomplicated point of view. The task of assignment involves knowing attitudes, including in some sense their 'strength,' and the force of the impact of each suggestion under consideration as tending to change them. Diffidence about analyzing matters of 'attitude' would become us, for there are indications that merely agreeing upon a scientific content for the term might keep sociologists busy for some time. However, it appears that an attitude rests upon at least these underlying factors: a value system, the 'brute' elements provided by the senses, and theories relating to these elements. Thus, basic to assigning 'probabilities' would be a knowledge, with respect to each person affecting the adoption of a policy, of how these factors combine in him to form attitudes, including what is the 'marginal influence' of changes in the respective factors. Given such information, successful forecasting would require discerning also exactly what persons the advice would reach and in what form and, for each person reached, just what changes would occur in each of his attitude-making factors. (Since forecasts are, for the purposes in question, to run in terms of probability distributions, the knowledge required – whatever its nature – would be more rather than less complex than these statements suggest.)

In the case of an official economic adviser to one or a few immediate determiners of policy, presumably sufficient knowledge for a forecast might be possessed – although it would be naïve to take for granted that the enigma which man presents to man regularly yields to the degree of intimacy involved in such a relationship. However, to assay how appropriately the cited requirements might in general give pause to a forecaster, it would be well to recall what must be meant by 'lines of action' open to economists as social advisers. These vary greatly as to immediacy of impact upon policy, ranging from the report of an official adviser, through systematic promotion (honest propaganda), down to a mere planting of seeds of thought whether in the classroom or in casual conversation. Evidently the overwhelming majority of 'actions' exercise their effects quite indirectly. What is the 'probability' that a policy-influencing marginal change in attitudes will result from planting an idea, or the means of arriving at good ideas, in the classroom or in an address or in social intercourse? With what degree of immediacy both in point of time and in point of the number of immediate impacts? A mere showing of difficulty would not invalidate the conception of a 'probability' approach. But it would scarcely be extreme to suspect that estimates of 'probability' would in the case of most expressions of espousal have a probable error so large as to render them 'statistically' insignificant. The knowledge stipulated as necessary was not characterized as sufficient for the appraisal of 'probabilities'. Indeed, contemplation suggests some mystery about the very nature of such a process in the kind of universe in question. These facts suggest a problem which for emphasis we may single out as our third point: a fundamental difficulty in the very notion of 'probability' as a property of the force of a piece of advice. Unless the intent is simply to lead others to act under false impression of the results to be expected, advice consists of making evident the soundness of an idea and relying upon the resulting recognition of that soundness to cause action based upon it. The force at work changing attitudes is, then, 'idea force'. 'Probability' implies a mechanical relation, some kind of quantitative continuity. But correct conclusions cannot flow from treating 'idea force' as if the law of conservation of energy applied to it; for, however an idea may get into a mind, it is capable of dying there or of gathering immense force. Moreover, a number of minds can be seeded with one expression of the idea. Potentially, them, the force may grow at an astronomical rate. All the determinants of whether it dies or gathers strength in a particular mind, we simply do not know. We do know, however, that which is believed to be true has an appeal to the mind believing it, over and above the attraction it may have on other grounds: truth has a positive appeal in its own right. Although other appeals may swamp this one, there is no limit to the possibilities of its breaking through and causing action. The degree of apparent influence of the person holding an idea is, therefore, no measure of the potential effect of his giving utterance to it. If there is one belief fundamental to, and universal in, our culture, it is this notion that truth as such has power. Such justification as may exist for the hope of a better world lies here and here only. In the face of these considerations it seems doubtful not merely whether we can effectively measure 'probabilities' for different 'actions' upon attitudes, but indeed whether any real meaning attaches to the conception.

In the fourth place, to guide oneself by a 'probability' calculus is one thing, but to say then that all persons should do likewise is to fall little if at all short of nonsense. There might be some sort of rationality to urging that others espouse according to value weights only, so as to leave one or a few free to add the 'probability' factor. The latter procedure implies estimating the current division of the forces of espousal and deciding whether one's own influence would suffice to change an inferior force into a superior. Evidently, then, much of the force exercised by others must have been somehow committed. If all, however, follow the 'probability' principle, no one can commit himself until many others (nearly all?) have committed themselves. Thus, for keeping public affairs relatively free from the influence of the disinterested, the 'probability' principle would be a reasonably effective device.

Since it would seem harsh to attribute to the 'realist' a meaning so patently foolish, an attempt at a different interpretation may be appropriate. Although the inference does not appear obviously logical, could the actual meaning involve a processing in which the many individual advisers, each with the 'probability' factor in mind, somehow simultaneously determine their respective positions? If so, to be sure, the implications are still not attractive. Major economic policy, in so far as it is influenced at all by economists, apparently ought to be the product of infinite involutions of guesses by each about what others are guessing about what he is guessing about what they will advocate! However, for example, having advocated farm-price supports on grounds of their 'probability,' it appears that one may take a fearless stand in favor of ninety per cent of parity as opposed to ninety-five percent – unless, indeed, the probabilities are too much against that. It is a depressing picture of the rôle of representatives of that higher learning upon which much of the hope of social improvement has sometimes been supposed to depend.

In view of the preceding point, a fifth one is evident: the 'probability' approach rests upon an ethical atomism which might reasonably be supposed long ago to have been barred by a well-established principle of ethics, that a precept is unacceptable for one man unless it would have an acceptable outcome when followed by all. In the face of this principle, how can the degree of immediate influence of a scholar upon practical affairs be deemed a matter of greater concern than the desirability of the direction of such influence as he does wield?

A sixth and major indictment of the 'probability' approach, although contained in much of the preceding discussion, should be made explicit. Fundamental to such a procedure is the fact that, while believing one course to be the best, I say or allow it to be thought that I believe a different one to be the best. That is to say, the approach explicitly calls for the active or passive concealment of truth. It should scarcely be necessary to argue against an idea which so patently strikes at the foundations of scientific integrity.

If the thoughts assembled here are sound, men will best serve the cause of social welfare if they refrain both from disposing of opponents as 'unrealistic,' in our defined sense, and from bowing to fear of that charge in selecting their own positions on policy. Degrees of 'probability' are incommensurable with degrees of value, and ethical considerations do not permit the former to outweigh the latter. The assignment of 'probabilities,' even with a highly oversimplified conception of their meaning, would in the great majority of cases be so difficult as to become absurd. The nature of 'idea force,' moreover, makes it doubtful whether any real meaning attaches to the very notion of 'probabilities of success' of different lines of advice and whether, therefore, there can be any such weights to superimpose upon value weights. In any case, to call the 'probability' approach proper for all who take a position on policy would be to advocate a practice which would remove any rational basis which 'probability' estimates might be imagined to have, by reducing all policy position-taking to a logically impossible universal mutual anticipation ending only in universal support of the status quo (in so far as change depends on deliberate human planning) and which would of course divorce policy selection from reference to value. Finally, the required concealment of truth is intolerable to the most fundamental conception of the scholar's reason for being. The 'probability' approach must surely be rejected, to say nothing of its being considered prerequisite to respectability. Only one type of serious defense of a policy is open to an economist or anyone else: he must maintain that the policy is good. True 'realism' is the same thing men have always meant by wisdom: to decide the immediate in the light of the ultimate. The economist must follow this ideal as best he can – in humility and in readiness to compare notions both of technical relations and of ultimate values.

Notes

1. At the time this article was first published in 1953 Philbrook was associate professor of economics at the University of North Carolina. He expressed thanks for criticism and stimulating discussion to Mr. George M. Woodward, Major Robert L. Bunting, Dr. Edwin J. Stringham, and Professor Dudley J. Cowden.

2. Throughout this paper the word 'advice' and terms used synonymously are to be interpreted in the broadest possible sense – to include any recommendation, inside or outside the classroom, made without hypothetical purpose clauses more restrictive than the necessarily implied aim to achieve the desirable.

6 How To Do Well While Doing Good!*

Gordon Tullock

Economic research always has the potential of contributing to public welfare since improved knowledge can have an effect on the world that is desirable and is unlikely to have an effect that is undesirable. Nevertheless, I would estimate that the average article in economic journals these days has very little prospect of contributing to the well-being of the world. Most economists know this and worry more about publication and tenure than about the contribution their research will make to public welfare. The argument of this chapter is that virtue does not have to be its own reward. The average economist can benefit his career while simultaneously making a contribution to the public welfare.

Consider, for example, the case of the dissolution of the Civil Aeronautics Board (CAB). In 1937, Congress cartelized the US air transport industry, establishing a government agency, the CAB, to supervise and control the cartel. As a result, in the United States air transportation prices were held well above their equilibrium, even though they were lower than the prices charged internationally and in Europe.[1]

In 1984, the CAB was abolished, and it is clear that economists played a major part in its destruction. A group of economists (Jim Miller is the one that I know best) devoted a great deal of time and effort to economic research in connection with the airline industry and to

---

* First published in David C. Colander (ed.), *Neoclassical Political Economy: The Analysis of Rent-Seeking and DUP Activities* (Cambridge, Mass.: Ballinger, 1984), pp. 229–40.

87

what we may call public relations activities in connection with it. They formed an improbable political alliance between the American Enterprise Institute and Senator Kennedy for the purpose of bringing the control device to an early grave. Further, they were able to convince some of the airlines that they would gain from the elimination of the CAB.

As far as I can see, when these economists began their campaign there was substantially no public interest in the matter at all; most people and politicians would have argued that the CAB was necessary in order to prevent the airlines from exploiting the passengers. It is also true that most of the economists who looked at the problem had approved the regulation. It should be said that a good many of the economists that looked at it were members of that small subset of the profession who were professional public utility economists and whose own personal income depends very heavily on the continued existence of these boards for which they can give expert testimony. Miller could have joined this small group but chose the other side, and in view of his subsequent career, it is hard to argue that he was not right, both from the standpoint of the public interest and his own career.

I do not want to, indeed am not competent to, go into the detailed history of this successful campaign, but I should like to point out two important factors: the first is that the average citizen, if he or she had known the truth about the CAB, would always have been opposed to it. This is one of the reasons why you can argue that it was in the public interest. The second is that it was not too hard to get the actual story out. The problem was mainly that of explaining the matter to the politician and the media. This is not necessarily easy since neither of these groups has any particular motive to think hard about the true public interest. They are both much more interested in the image of public interest currently in the minds of the citizenry. But to say that it is not easy, is not to say that it is impossible, and here we have a clear-cut case where it was accomplished. The theme of this sermon is 'Go Thou and Do Likewise'.

The CAB is not by any means the only example. Banking regulation has to a large extent collapsed in recent years. This was to a considerable extent the result of technological developments, but the existence of a vigorous group of economic critics of the regulations was no doubt important. After all, the regulators could have just changed their regulations to take in the new technology. The fact that they did not was certainly, to some extent, the result of the work of the anti-regulation economists in this area. The partial deregulation of the trucking industry is almost entirely he result of economic activity and, indeed, during the latter part of the Carter administration an economist was acting chairman of the Interstate Commerce Commission (ICC).[2]

In all of the cases originally the majority of the economic profession was on the wrong side, *favoring* regulation. This is one of the problems we face when we talk about economists having a good effect on policy. We must admit that in the past economists have frequently had a bad effect. Good economists have always had a good effect, however, and those who had a bad effect were bad economists. This is not just an *ad hoc* argument; I believe that one can look into the matter and discover that the people who favored such agencies as the ICC at the time they were set up were markedly poorer economists than the ones who objected to it.

There are other striking examples. In 1929 the United States was probably the world's highest tariff nation. It is true that during the intervening years we have developed a habit of setting up quotas and voluntary agreements, but even if you add those on, we still are a very low trade barrier nation. This change seems to be almost entirely an outcome of steady economic criticism. Certainly, it is very hard to put your finger on any other reason for the change.

Once again however, the history is not clear. The protective tariff, of course, has long been a *bête noire* of the economists, but a review of the advanced theoretical literature over the last years shows far more discussion of optimal tariffs than of the desirability of getting rid of tariffs. This is particularly surprising because the articles dealing with optimal tariffs rarely, if ever, point out that their optimality is a rather special one and that, in any event, it would be impossible to calculate an optimal tariff in the real world.[3] Still, the majority of economic opinion was always against protective tariffs even if this point of view did not get much attention in the technical journals. In a way the success of the tariff-lowering movement depended a great deal on the fact that the secretary of state for some twelve years was a former southern congressman who had learned free trade in his youth and stuck with it. Cordell Hull, of course, has been dead for many years, but the trend that he started continued. Certainly, the general favorable economic climate for such cuts was important there.

What can we do now and, more specifically, what can readers do that is good but will also help them in their careers? My argument is that there are numerous instances that almost all economists can agree are rent-seeking and detract from general welfare. In such cases virtue need not be its own reward.

AN EXAMPLE OF AN ANTI-RENT-SEEKING ARGUMENT

Let me begin with an example on which almost all economists would agree. There are about 300 British Columbian egg producers, and some time ago it occurred to them that they were not as wealthy as they would like to be. They pressed the British Columbia government into setting up the British Columbia Egg Control Board, a cartel in which the government not only fixed prices but actually engaged in civil service employing operations. Specifically, the Egg Control Board purchased the eggs from the owners of egg factories and then sold them to the public.

The original arguments for this program (other than that it would make the egg producers wealthy), were that they would stabilize prices and protect the 'family farm'.

They have stabilized prices. If you compare prices in British Columbia to those in Washington State, which has roughly the same conditions, it is clear they fluctuate more in Washington State. However, they have stabilized prices primarily by preventing the falls in price that periodically cause so much distress for producers of eggs in Washington. Whether this particular kind of stability is admired by the housewife, as opposed to the egg producer, is not pellucidly clear. As for protecting the 'family farmer,' I doubt that these enterprises really should be referred to as family farms, but it is true that there is some evidence that the average size is possibly slightly suboptimal in British Columbia.

In order to charge a monopoly price it is, of course, necessary to prevent entry into the business. This is done by the traditional grandfather clause, so that those who are producing eggs in British Columbia when the scheme started are the only ones who are permitted to do so. As a result, the wealth of the farmers has increased very greatly because the permits to produce eggs are now valuable. Indeed, for the average egg producer, the permit is more than half his total capitalization.

It should be pointed out, however, that in addition to the egg producers there is one other beneficiary of this scheme. The egg producers produce more eggs than can be sold in British Columbia at what the British Columbia Egg Marketing Board thinks is a stable price. The additional eggs are sold on the international market for conversion to things like dried eggs at whatever the market will bring.

How do I know all of this about the British Columbia Egg Marketing Board? The answer is simple. Two economists decided that it would be a worthwhile study and the Fraser Institute published it in the form of a small booklet.[4] Borcherding and Dorosh thus acquired a reasonably good publication, probably quite easily. It is no criticism of the pamphlet to say that it involves no particular economic sophistication or advanced techniques. It may have been a little difficult, because I presume the Egg

Board was not exactly enthusiastic about cooperating with them. Nevertheless, I would imagine that the cost/benefit analysis of this pamphlet, in terms of getting a publication and the effort put into it, was very exceptionally favorable. Further, the pamphlet itself certainly will make the survival of the Egg Board, at least, a little less certain, a result most economists believe would be beneficial.

Of course I hope that more is done here. The pamphlet was published by the Fraser Institute, which exists essentially for the purpose of doing this kind of thing and attempting to influence public policy by its research. The head of the Fraser Institute frequently appears on television. I would think that the prospects for the Egg Board are clearly worse than they were before all of this started. I hope that Borcherding and Dorosh follow up on this, not so much by further research (although that of course probably can be done) as by trying to get other publications in the local media.

Here, I am going to suggest that they do something unprofessional; I believe economists should make an active effort to interest the local newspaper and other media in such issues. Stories of a small entrenched interest robbing the general public are the kind of story that does go well once you sell a reporter. Further, they are not particularly complicated.

Such activities are not the ones economists normally engage in; moreover, it will be a little difficult to interest newspaper reporters. Newspaper reporters tend simply to say what other newspaper reporters have said.[5] Granted that reporters behave this way, they are nonetheless normally looking for a scandal which they can make headlines about, and there are innumerable examples. The licensing of private yacht salesmen in California is my favorite case of the public being protected against low commission rates, but I am sure most economists can think of a half dozen more. But let us defer further discussion of general publicity for now.

We can roughly divide various rent-seeking activities for which there is likely a consensus among economists that they are indeed rent-seeking into three categories: those that involve spending money in a way that in the standpoint of the average taxpayer is foolish but that benefits a particular group, those that involve fixing prices above equilibrium, and those that involve obtaining cartel profits by restricting entry into a business.[6]

Economists have not been very successful in their efforts to stop federal government expenditures resulting from rent-seeking. Jack Hirshleifer, for example, devoted a good deal of time and energy, together with a number of experts in the field, in attempting to prevent the Feather River Project from being built in California. It has not been completed yet, but, on the whole, their efforts cannot be said to have made a major impact. I do not know why it is harder to stop government expenditures of this sort than the other kinds of government activity, but I suspect the problem is simply that from the standpoint of the citizens of California, the project is in fact a good one.[7] Their efforts were very largely concentrated in California. The cost, on the other hand, was very largely borne outside California. There has been relatively little in the way of efforts on the part of economists to stop locally financed expenditures where I think they could have more impact. In making attacks on local expenditures, I think it is wise to keep in mind that in many cases the money actually is federal. It is not unwise of the local government to accept a gift from the national government even if the gift is not in optimal form. The conclusion that can be drawn is that rent-seeking can most often be stopped if the groups that are bearing the cost can be informed.

Turning to the other two categories, entry restriction and price control, most of these are state and local regulations, although there are, of course, federal examples. At these lower levels of government the beneficiaries and the injured groups are somewhat closer together and informing the injured group is somewhat easier. Further, an individual's activities are more likely to have effect in such a restricted area, and last but not least, most of these projects are fairly simple. Thus, it seems better to concentrate anti-rent-seeking activities in these areas.

Let us begin with the cases in which the prices are fixed by some government board, with a maximum and minimum price. This is essentially the British Columbia Egg Board, and there is a simple argument to be used against it, which is that there should be no minimum price. Consumers can hardly be protected by a minimum price. If you can get the minimum price out, the pressure group that set the thing up in the first place will probably see to it that the maximum price is eliminated.

At this point, I should perhaps mention the standard rationalization,[8] that advocates of the minimum price will almost certainly use. They will allege that if the minimum price is not imposed then some company with a lot of money will cut prices, drive the competition out of business, and then exploit its monopoly. This argument is eliminated by not arguing against the maximum price, and instead leaving that to the regular political process. The lesson here is a simple one: the best economic reasoning is not always (indeed, it is generally not) the best politics. Policy economists must formulate arguments that are most liable to lead to the desired outcome, not that are most elegant.

Restrictions on entry are subject to a variety of forms of arguments. The formal rationalization – that is, that they make certain that the service provided is on a certain level of quality – can be countered by Milton Friedman's 'certification,' which is that the state or local government could provide certificates of competence to anyone who passed their regulations, but not prohibit people who do not have such certificates from practicing provided that there was no fraud. In other words, the person without a certificate would not tell people who solicited his services that he had one. This procedure would probably eliminate most of the monopoly gains and convert the present arrangements into something that might even be socially desirable.

The usual argument against this, of course, is that people are not bright enough even to look at the certificate. (Why people who argue this way think that people are bright enough to vote, I don't know, but they do.) To counter this argument one can move to a second line of defense, by pointing out that these regulations are not (and, in fact, make very little effort to pretend to be) efforts to raise the quality of services.

Uniformly, when such restrictions are put on, everyone now in the trade is grandfathered in. Indeed, this is the reason they are put on – the current people in the trade want to have their lifetime income raised by reducing competition. Clearly, if everybody now in the trade is competent without investigation of any sort, it is unlikely that an investigation is of any use. Thus, all new proposals of this sort can be opposed quite readily.

If we turn to the older ones, there may well be an examination, usually an irrelevant examination, but the examination is given only to new entrants. The appropriate argument here is simply that it is possible for a person practicing, whether as a doctor or as a plumber, to fail to keep up with new developments, forget old developments, or, for that matter, become dipsomaniac. It would be desirable, therefore, that everyone in the trade not only be examined when he enters but be reexamined from time to time. It is hard to think of any argument against this, but it clearly would eliminate the political pressure for the restriction if the restriction had to take the form of continuing examinations.

Finally, there is a constitutional argument. The Supreme Court has held that requiring a waiting period for a new entrant into a state before he can go on relief violates his constitutional rights to travel freely. Prohibiting him from practicing his trade as a carpenter would also do so. Of course, if the restriction were literally evenhanded – that is, if the New York restriction on carpentry is the same for New Yorkers as for Californians who want to migrate to New York – then this constitutional argument would not exist. Such a restriction, however, would imply that if all people who are practicing carpentry in New York at the time the law was passed are admitted without examination, people who are practicing carpentry in other states at that time should also be admitted without examination. If we could get the Supreme Court to hold that this is what the Constitution said, we could feel confident that there would be absolutely no political effort to establish new restrictions on entry in the states and local governments throughout the United States.

If an examination for carpenters has been in existence for a long time so that there are not very many carpenters from other states who were carpenters at the time that the original carpenters were grandfathered in, there is a somewhat more difficult constitutional problem. Here, however, an argument would be needed that the examination is not really intended to certify people's ability as carpenters but to prevent migration from other states. It seems to me that the simple fact that the examination is not given regularly to people who are already practicing in order to make certain that they are retaining their skills, and not becoming dipsomaniacs, would be adequate here. Such constitutional arguments may or may not be successful in the courts. I recommend their use in economic arguments, even though they are not strictly relevant, simply because I think they will have a persuasive effect on the average voter.

In making any anti-rent-seeking argument, one should always point out that the data are inadequate (one can also imply in a tactful manner, that the reason that the data are inadequate is that the guilty are concealing or keeping secret evidence of their guilt). More data are always needed and generally the pressure group is to some extent unwilling to provide data because it fears strengthening your argument. Mainly, however, this argument places you in a very good position for rebuttal. Almost certainly, the pressure group representatives will argue that you are simply ignorant in their field. A response in which you say that your ignorance is partly because they are keeping secrets and ask them to provide further information generally would be helpful. In the unlikely event that they do provide additional information, of course, you have opportunity for further and better research.

A second argument that inevitably can be made is that the pressure group has something material to gain from its activities. Although we, as economists, do not regard this as in any way discreditable, the average person does. In fact, the pressure group will normally be arguing that its existence benefits people it in fact injures, but it will normally not deny that its own members are gaining, too. You will thus merely be giving strong emphasis to something the pressure group tends to pass over lightly.

If individual economists would select some blatantly undesirable activity, preferably a state or local government, and become a modest expert on it, it is my contention that the economy would improve. Doing so does not involve a major investment. In general, these programs are not complicated, but nevertheless becoming an expert will involve some work. After becoming an expert, the economist should attempt to get media publicity for the position with the result first, of certainly attracting the attention of the pressure group, which may or may not be useful, and, second, if the economist pushes hard enough and is persistent, he probably will have at least some effect on the activity of the pressure group.

Here I should emphasize that though I am suggesting this as an individual effort, there is no reason why small collectives of economists should not be involved, and there is certainly no reason why you should not seek out the support of other groups. The League of Women Voters, for example, tends to go about looking for good causes and you may be able to improve their taste. There are also various business groups, Rotary Clubs, and so on that are always on the lookout for a lecturer and that would give you an opportunity to provide some influence.

Persistence will, however, be necessary. The pressure group will continue and a mere couple of months' noise about it is helpful but unlikely to accomplish a great deal. Persistence is not difficult, however. Once you have passed the threshold of knowing enough about the organization so that you can regard yourself as a modest expert, it is very easy to keep up with further developments and incorporate additional data into your analyses. Further, your contacts with the media are apt to be self-reinforcing. After you have convinced people that you know a great deal about, let us say, controls on egg production, you are likely to find television program directors asking you questions about all economic matters. You should answer them, of course, to the best of your ability, and this will not only, we hope, contribute to the economic information of the public but also give media representatives an idea of your expertise so that when you bring up the subject of eggs or whatever it is, they are likely to pay attention.

Most economists only occasionally give lectures to something like the Rotary Club. I am suggesting that this aspect of professional life be sharply increased. Furthermore, I am suggesting that you become an expert on some rather obscure topic instead of giving your lecture to the Rotary Club on what is right or what is wrong with Reaganomics. This is indeed a change from the normal academic life but not a gigantic one. I am not suggesting that you devote immense amounts of time to these joint projects, merely that you do indeed devote some time to them. In a way it may be a pleasant change from the more profound and difficult work that I am sure mainly occupies your time.

So far I have been telling you how you can do good and have not explained why I think you can also do well. The first thing to be said is that of course the kind of research I am proposing does have some potential for publication in the regular economic literature. *The Journal of Law and Economics*, *The Journal of Political Economy*, *Public Policy*, and others all are interested in such articles. I would also suggest that the political science journals would be interested, although it would be necessary to make a few changes in your approach if you submitted articles to them.

However, while all of these people would be interested and, I think, the prospects for publication are quite good, it has to be said that if a great many economists begin working in this area it would rapidly exhaust the desire for such articles in these journals. After a while, only the very best of such articles could be published there. Further, in this case 'best' would not refer entirely to the quality of the work but also to the importance of the subject matter. A new twist in cartel economics would, for example, probably be publishable when hundreds of studies of specific cartels would not.

So far, of course, the tolerance of these journals for this kind of article has by no means been exhausted and those of you who get in first could no doubt take advantage of that tolerance. Once we turn from this kind of journal publication, however, there are a number of other places with gradually decreasing prestige where you can get published. There is now a chain of economic institutes who are in general interested in studies of this kind of cartel.[9] The Borcherding and Dorosh pamphlet is a good example. Clearly this is a perfectly suitable publication to put on your vitae even if it does not carry quite so much weight as publication in *The Journal of Political Economy* (JPE). I, as a matter of fact, have three such things on my own vitae. Indeed, I would imagine that in cost/benefit terms these things are considerably more highly paying than JPE articles because although the payoff is not as high, the cost of producing them is also low.

Below that level there is the possibility of fairly widespread publication in such things as articles in local newspapers, letters to the editor, and so on. These are not great publications and you might want to indicate on your bibliography that you think they are not. For example, you could have a separate section for newspaper articles and letters to the editor. You might even mention your appearances on television in this separate section.

With respect to these less important articles, speeches, and the like, the payoff in academic life is, of course, quite low per unit. Most universities, however, regard activity in the public arena as meritorious and pay it off in higher wages. It also carries with it the advertising value that an article in *The Journal of Political Economy* carries, although, once again, at a lower level.

Although these are less important publications, their cost is also quite low. Once you have become an expert in this area you could grind them out practically at will, producing a letter to the editor, for example, in a half-hour. Thus, once again, the cost-benefit analysis from a pure career standpoint seems to be positive.

This may immediately raise a question in your mind. How do I know that better information is likely to cause the end of these special-interest arrangements? After all, they have been in existence a long time and most economists know about them in general even if the public does not. They do not seem to be very secretive. I believe that they depend on either ignorance or misinformation on the part of the public. My reasons for believing so are two: first, if you discuss any of them with average voters it will turn out that they have never heard of them, or if they have heard of them, they are badly misinformed about them. In the case of the British Columbia Egg Board, the average voter probably does not know that there is such an organization. The voter who does probably has bought the argument that the organization stabilizes prices and protects the family farm.

However, in addition to this informal public opinion poll, there is another and, in my opinion, more important reason. If we think of the British Columbia Egg Board, any economist could quickly arrange a set of taxes on eggs together with direct subsidies to the people who were in the business of producing eggs[10] that would make both the customers and the producers of the eggs better off. We do not see this direct subsidy being used. Why do pressure groups not simply aim at a low tax on the entire population that is used to pay a direct sum of money to them rather than these clearly non-Pareto-optimal arrangements that we in fact observe? I think the only available explanation for this is that they know that a certain amount of confusion and misdirection is necessary. A direct cash transfer, a tax of $10 per family in British Columbia for the purpose of paying a pension to the 300 people who happen to own egg factories at the time the program was put into effect, would never go through because it is too blatant and obvious. It is necessary that these things be covered by some kind of deception. Granted that I am right about this – that these programs require that the people be misinformed – informing them is likely to terminate the program. No politician is going to tax all of his constituents a small sum of money in order to give a large sum of money to a small group no matter how well organized that small group is if everyone knows that is what he is doing. Economists can see to it that they do know.

Note here, also, that the nature of the mass media is on your side. The mass media all aim at large audiences. The small pressure group does not have much chance of getting the attention of the mass media except, possibly, unfavorable attention. The small pressure group very likely has its own journal, which it uses for internal communication, but the owner of a television station or a newspaper will tend to come down for his customers *en masse*, not a tiny minority of his customers. Thus, not only is secrecy and deception necessary here but the nature of the mass media means that unmasking of these villains is likely to be popular with those who want to make money in the media business.

I am sure all of this sounds rather wild to most of you. I gave an earlier version of this chapter at my own university and a young ABD ['all but dissertation' – a graduate who only has to submit a dissertation to obtain a degree], who had been listening and apparently could not believe his ears came up afterward and asked me whether it was really true that I was suggesting that he not only study up on some local government-managed cartel but seek publication in places other than the JPE. I assured him that was my objective. He went away looking astounded, not, I think, at the brilliance of my ideas, but at the eccentricity.

This particular young man will, I think, have great difficulty getting any publications ever in the JPE. Competition is stiff (even to this day I have about half of my submissions turned down[11]), and most economists will never get a single article published in a leading journal. Still, I assume all of you are members of that small minority who do occasionally break into print in such places as JPE, the AER [*American Economic Review*], and the QJE [*Quarterly Journal of Economics*].

Turning to the problem of the man who does have great difficulty getting anything published, something on his vita is better than nothing, and the proposal that I am making is a way in which he can pretty much guarantee he will have at least something on his vita. For the more productive economist, who does currently produce articles for the leading journals, it is still helpful to add additional items even if these additional items are not of Nobel Prize quality. Once again, the cost of producing these things is comparatively low, so you make a good deal per unit of effort.

Even if there were no beneficial impact on your career, nevertheless I would urge it on you. All of us are, to some minor extent, charitable and this is a particularly convenient way for economists to work out their charitable feelings. Getting rid of the British Columbia Egg Board might not impress you as a major accomplishment, but individuals can expect to have only small impacts on the massive structure that we call modern society. It is likely that you will do more good for the world by concentrating on abolishing some such organization in your locality than the average person does – indeed, very much more. It is an unusual form of charity, but a form in which the payoff would be high. But although such work falls squarely in the path of virtue, it also has positive payoffs. You can, to repeat my title, do well while you are doing good.

Notes

1. The apparent reason that American airlines' prices were lower than those in Europe was not that our airlines were any less monopolistic but that they were more efficient, with the result that the optimum monopoly price for them was lower than the optimum monopoly price for such monsters of inefficiency as Air France or Japan Airlines.

2. Unfortunately, this partial deregulation seems to have stopped. (I hope temporarily.) Once again, it is encouraging that most economists were opposed to this regulation.

3. It is not that the optimal tariff literature is wrong. It is that it can be misused and that economists are more likely to have a positive effect on public policy because rent-seeking forces will be pushing for a tariff that is far beyond any optimal tariff.

4. The booklet is *The Egg Marketing Board, A Case Study of Monopoly and Its Social Costs*, by Thomas Borcherding and Gary W. Dorosh (Vancouver: The Fraser Institute, 1981).

5. The 'deregulation' that has been so successful in recent years in the United States is an example. It has become more or less a fad with most of the correspondents for *The Washington Post* who were in favor of it without having any clear idea why.

6. I leave aside here those cases in which if we look only at the short run, as unfortunately the voter does, the beneficiaries outnumber the people who pay. Price controls on gas are a current example.

7. Ignoring, of course, those particular farmers who will be damaged by the canal across the delta.

8. I encountered it in high school.

9. The bulk of them owe their origin to the energies of Anthony Fisher.

10. Some of these might, of course, decide to stop producing eggs and move to Hawaii on the subsidy.

11. I have a large collection of unpublished articles.

7 The Common Weal and Economic Stories*

D. N. McCloskey

The worldly philosophers change the world with their stories and metaphors. There's work for the econo-literary critic in showing how the rhetoric matters to policy and in distinguishing the good stories of policy from the bad. (Robert Boynton, among other things a politico-literary critic, has done so for the Senate Agriculture Committee [1987].)

The stories in economics are numerous beyond count. The moral outrage that fuels some of them is surprising in so desiccated a science. Since its beginning economics has reserved its second greatest indignation for monopolists (its greatest is for clumsy governments). When most economists think of American doctors, for example, they think of monopoly. On the face of it the analogy does not look persuasive. After all, there are hundreds of thousands of doctors, not one, so in no literal sense does the medical profession constitute one seller. Medicine talks about itself in noncommercial terms, as a disinterested science and a sacrificing profession. The economists see it differently, largely because of the story they tell.[1] Once upon a time (namely, until the 1930s) medical doctors in the United States earned roughly the same as lawyers or middle management. Then, beginning about 1910 and concluding by about World War II, through their state boards of medical examiners and the corruption of state legislatures, the doctors seized control of the supply of

---

* First published as chapter 11 of *If You're So Smart: The Narrative of Economic Expertise* (Chicago: University of Chicago Press, 1990), pp. 150–62.

health care, closing medical schools, forbidding foreign doctors to immigrate, and preventing nurses, pharmacists, and others from practicing medicine, at just the time that medicine began to cure more people than it killed. The result was an astonishing increase in the relative income of American doctors (not matched in places like Britain or Italy where the doctors did not succeed in blockading entry), who now earn three times what comparable professionals earn, happily ever after. The economist views the behavior of the American Medical Association as union power more effective than that of plumbers and electricians, concealed behind a myth of self-sacrifice and a façade of ethical purpose. The economic story results in shockingly harsh ethical judgments about the American doctor. A bus driver, says the economist, holds the lives of more people in his hands; a lawyer works longer hours; a professor studies more. But the doctor exploits the most tax shelters, putting medical care out of the reach of the poor.

Economists have developed over the past twenty years or so a similar story about regulation, which, like the medical story, they teach to their students as gospel. What is notable is the change in attitude. Economists once retold the Progressive story, assuming without irony that regulators would be able to defy politics for the good of the community. Prohibition, the city manager movement, and especially the regulation of monopoly were all favorites of American economists in the first two decades of the century. The Progressive program was of course put into practice by the New Deal and by the Great Society programs of the 1960s. But since those Progressive times the economists have changed their story.

In the new story, the Interstate Commerce Commission (ICC), for example, is said to have been taken over by the very railroads it was supposed to regulate shortly after its formation in 1887 (and later by the big trucking firms). The hero of the Progressive story, a selfless regulator protecting the little man from big business, has for two decades raised increasingly derisive laughter in the halls of economics departments. The economist asks with a smirk: 'Do you really expect United Van Lines to sit idly by while the ICC guts its profit?' The moral authority of one regulatory commission after another has been undermined in the eyes of economists by the new story line (lately, for example, the Security and Exchange Commission[2]). The results show in deregulation, an example of the power of ideas as against vested interests. Ideas, not dollars, conquered the regulatory agencies. Many of the agencies were in fact infiltrated by economists educated at universities like Chicago and UCLA, which had long been telling the anti-regulatory tale. The economist's story has become the law.

The story of monopoly, to take a related example, was told for a long time in economics as a story of 'structure, conduct and performance'. That is, monopoly was viewed as rain, some of which must fall upon each society. Markets came with 'structures' of one seller or two sellers or many sellers, causeless and natural. The job of the economist was to provide umbrellas for the victims of the bad performance. Until the 1970s every course outside the University of Chicago and a few other places in 'industrial organization' (the field of economics that studies monopoly and competition) told this tale: monopoly just happens and the economist just stops it. Since the 1970s a new and richer story of monopoly has been told, of how a monopoly comes to be a monopoly, and what therefore is to be done about each separate history. The new theories are casuistical, argued case by case under principles that cannot be applied as invariant rules. If a monopoly of computers arises from one of many potential competitors, for example, it may not be desirable to regulate it, since the disciplining threat of new entry remains.

The analogous case is slum clearance, a long-standing policy of enlightened nations. Slums are bad relative to ideal communities, of course, just as a monopoly is bad relative to an ideal industry. The instinct of the social engineer is therefore to clear the slums and break up the monopoly. But the result has commonly been the concentration of the poor into housing projects worse than the original slums, and the concentration of political pressure into regulatory commissions more monopolistic than the monopolies. The causes of slums reassert themselves in the Robert Taylor Homes along the Dan Ryan Expressway in Chicago, since the housing was not itself a cause. So too in the regulation of monopoly: when monopoly is caused by the exercise of political power, as it often is, putting politics in charge of the industry is not going to help. The political economy asserts itself in the golden rule, that those who have the gold, rule.

The stories of economics matter to all manner of economic policy. Consider the story of helping poor countries, whose minimal plot is: once the poor countries were poor, then the rich countries helped them, and now they too are rich. Peter Bauer, an Austrian-British economist who has long criticized the ruling metaphors in this story, has now the satisfaction of seeing his grimmest prediction come true.[3] As he feared some decades ago, the advice of economists has on balance hurt the poor countries of the world, hurting more as the quarrel over equality between 'The North' and 'The South' has intensified. Most of the followers have moved along the track, but notably slower than the leaders.

It is not surprising that an economics taking itself to be value-free social engineering should do a poor job in advising poor countries. Economics around 1950 gave up social philosophy and social history to become a blackboard subject. The poor countries provided convenient laboratories to try out what was discovered on the blackboard. The governments of western Europe proved wary of the snake oil, but other governments, and intergovernmental governments, lined up at the wagon to buy.

The result was a devaluation by intellectuals of voluntary exchange. After all, what is so fine about voluntary exchange if crushing it can produce the wealth of nations? And why should historical and philosophical doubts that the wealth arises from planning be entertained if a sweet diagram can prove that planning works? The planning and government programs worked badly, on the whole, as is suggested by the unraveling of Eastern Europe and the stagnation of South Asia and the long night of Africa. The postwar experiment with planning was a treason of the clerks, arising from their religion, an irrational belief in their ability to predict and control.

The metaphor of the 'Third World' itself was born (as Bauer has noted) with foreign aid and anti-communism shortly after the war. It asks a question of equity. Is it fair that the First World has all the riches? By the mere act of speaking of equity versus efficiency the economists import into the argument, as though it was uncontroversial, a utilitarian ethic. The audience is invited to think of tradeoffs between the one and the other. As the economists would say, mathproudly, $U = U$ (Efficiency, Equity) in which Efficiency is the size of national income and Equity is measured by the distribution of income. This is not 'wrong'; it is simply one metaphor among many, some more apt for particular uses than others. If economists think of equity in such terms, for example, they will not ask how the Efficiency was achieved (by executing people jailed in football stadiums, say) or whether equity entails stealing from innocents (by executing people who buy low and sell high).

The North is meant to feel guilty that by the grace of God it gets more than the South. Bauer has treated at length the use of the notion of 'our' guilt as a justification for compulsory charity. Clergymen and upper middle class intellectuals delight in the transformation of *mea culpa* into *nostra culpa*, prejudging in a word the weighty question of whether charity should be individual or social.

Bauer notes similarly the danger in the related metaphor of 'nation building,' a handsome neoclassical building in which political prisoners scream in the basement. The figure of a building treats people as 'lifeless bricks, to be moved by some master builder'.[4] Nation building is not merely a metaphor, mere ornamental rhetoric, but a political argument put into a word. The 'nation' is to be 'built' by the government, indeed by the present set of colonels and chieftains in charge of the building project.

The very word 'development' is a metaphor, of course, limiting our thinking at the same time it makes thinking possible. 'Economic growth' sounds better than 'economic change,' and 'change' better than 'losing existing jobs,' but they are translatable one into the other, suggesting different policies. Economists are not usually conscious of the difference the words make. A self-conscious metaphor has a different effect from an unself-conscious one. The economist and social thinker Mancur Olson has used comparisons among one-man boats, eight-man boats, and multi-oared galleys to illuminate the wealth of nations.[5] He uses the figure openly and self-consciously, and therefore the effect is merely communicative and ornamental. An explicit metaphor does not bite.

The word 'problem,' likewise, answers an economic question before one thinks to ask it. Many reputable economists argue for example that the balance-of-payments 'problem' is not a problem at all, in the sense of something requiring that 'we' find 'a solution'. No one would worry about the balance of payments if the statistics on it were not collected – which is not something that can be said about some other problems facing an economic community, such as poverty or inflation. Yet many people are exercised about The Problem and propose desperate remedies. The statistics led the British government during the 1950s and early 1960s to a policy of 'stop-go,' with lurching booms and governmentally-induced busts, damaging the British economy for the long run.

The nineteenth century invented the talk of a 'social *problem*,' an 'economic *problem*,' and so on, problems which finally the Great Geometer in London or Washington is to solve with compass and straightedge. The economic historian Max Hartwell speaks often of the rhetoric of British parliamentary inquiries in the nineteenth century as defining problems where no one had seen them before. It is not always done with mirrors, of course; this or that condition worthy of correction does exist. But in any case it is done with words. Someone who has persuaded you to speak of inequality of income as a problem has accomplished the most difficult part of her task. In particular, the array of metaphors taken from sport are crucial to the solving of problems. Sporting metaphors present themselves as innocuous ornaments and are especially popular among Americans, who, good-hearted as they are, favor the happy notion that in a conflict no one really gets hurt (Europeans will use metaphors of war and conquest in similar cases). The ideal is team play, joining together to score a goal against the foreigner or in a more mellow way to 'achieve a personal goal'. Whenever we hear that 'we' should do such and such the signal has been raised: watch for the team metaphor in action.

The best that human frailty is likely to achieve along this line is a book on *The Zero-Sum Solution: Building a World-Class American Economy* by Lester Thurow,[6] an economist and dean of the business school at the Massachusetts Institute of Technology. It is an intelligent work from which much can be learned. The book illustrates how much economists agree and how much their agreement depends on their shared devotion to quantitative thinking, the metaphor of a set of accounts. The trouble lies in its metaphors in aid of storytelling. The book treats income and wealth throughout as being extracted like football yardage from non-Americans, especially Japanese and other Asian non-Americans. 'To play a competitive game is not to be a winner – every competitive game has its losers – it is only to be given a chance to win ... Free market battles can be lost as well as won, and the United States is losing them on world markets'.[7] One chapter is entitled 'Constructing an Efficient Team'. Thurow talks repeatedly about America 'competing' and 'beating' the rest of the world with a 'world-class economy'. At one point he complains that more people do not adopt his favored metaphor, which he calls 'reality': 'For a society which loves team sports ... it is surprising that Americans won't recognize the same reality in the far more important international economic game'.[8]

In more aggressive moods Thurow trades his football helmet for a flak jacket: 'American firms will occasionally be defeated at home and will not have compensating foreign victories'.[9] Foreign trade is viewed as the economic equivalent of war. Unsurprisingly, British journalists in the late nineteenth century spoke in identically bellicose terms about the American 'threat' and the German 'menace'. And in part, with due allowance for contingency, the competition for first place on the metaphorical battlefield of commerce led most gratifyingly to the literal battlefields of the Somme and Verdun.

Three metaphors govern Thurow's story: this metaphor of the 'international zero-sum game"; a metaphor of the domestic 'problem' that damages performance in the game; and a metaphor of 'we' who face the problem. *We* have a domestic *problem* of productivity that leads to a *loss* in the international *game*. Thurow has spent a long time interpreting the world with these linked metaphors (he has written other books using them, as have many journalists: Thurow is unusual only in being a good economist using such rhetoric). It is America's job to 'compete on world markets',[10] not to make itself wise and competent; what 'counts' in Japanese economic performance are its export industries,[11] not its wretchedly inefficient agriculture and retailing.

The subject, though, is the exchange of goods and services, Japanese automobiles for American timber, German steel tubes for Soviet natural gas. The game metaphor does not seem apt. If exchange is a game it resembles one in which everyone wins, like aerobic dancing. Trade in this view is *not* zero sum. It is positive sum. There are social, overall, mutual gains from trade. How does an economist know? Because the trade was voluntary. That's Adam Smith's metaphor.

To be sure, viewed from the factory floor the trade with Japan (or for that matter with Massachusetts or with the town over the hill) *is* zero sum, which gives Thurow's metaphor an air of common sense. To a businessperson 'fighting' Japanese competition in making automobiles, her loss is indeed Toyota's gain. (Thurow does not view California's competition against Massachusetts with the same alarm. When you think of it, this is strange. If the object is to preserve jobs in Massachusetts, then assembly plants in California or Tennessee are the main competition, the main taker of jobs, to use the noneconomist's way of saying it. Why pick on foreigners?)

The game-playing metaphor looks at only one side of the trade, the selling side. As Adam Smith remarked famously, 'Consumption is the sole end and purpose of all production; and the interest of the producer ought to be attended to, only so far as it may be necessary for promoting that of the consumer'.[12] Economists claim to see around and underneath the economy. They claim to do the accounts from the social point of view. Underneath it all (again: the economist's favorite metaphor) Jim Beam of Iowa trades with Tatsuro Saki of Tokyo. A Toyota sold to the USA pays for 2000 tons of soybeans bought by Japan. The mainstream economist's metaphor of mutual trade differs from that of the anti-economic economists, such as Friedrich List, the German theorist of the *Zollverein*, or Henry Carey, the American theorist of protection in the nineteenth century, or Lester Thurow.

'The heart of America's competitiveness problem is to be found in low productivity growth ... [Well-wishers of America] would have to advocate some form of industrial policy to cure the competitiveness problem'.[13] Problems have solutions, called 'policies' which 'we must adopt'. It is not hard to guess who the Solver is: I'm from the Government, and I'm here to solve your problem. The confidence in the ideas of economists and planners is hardly justified by experience. Do economists really know enough that planning for research and development, in imitation of the Japanese, should be handed over to a MITI-ish organization? Thurow speaks repeatedly of 'social organization': we can do better by conscious planning, says he, and of course we know the group of experts who should do the planning.

Thurow's metaphor gets its appeal from the story into which it fits. The story is the one imposed on late Victorian Britain: in the sunset of hegemony, Britain basked complacently while others hustled. American intellectuals are worried that something similar is about to happen to them. The same reply can be made: American income after all will continue to grow whether or not America continues to have the literal lead in income. (In any case, American growth has been slower than that of most countries for most of its history: like Britain, it started rich.)

And why would one wish American hegemony to be fastened on the world forever? Is it God's plan that the United States of America should ever after be top nation? Why should we wish relative poverty in perpetuity on our Chinese and Latin American friends? Is this what economic ethics leads us to? It is a finding of economic history that trade among rich nations is better for the rich nations than trade with poor countries.[14] In any case, one would think that the proper audience for policy would be a citizen of the world, not merely an American. What does it matter to me if my relatively wealthy neighbor in Virginia chooses to read too few good books? Shouldn't I care more about the appalling poverty of people in Bangladesh?

The answer is not obvious one way or the other. The claims of community have to be taken seriously. The appropriateness of a strictly nationalist rhetoric for policy, however, is seldom questioned. What is the ethically relevant community? Some years ago at the Institute for Advanced Study at Princeton the political scientist Joseph Carens gave a luncheon talk about his research on American immigration policy. The audience expected him to say that concerning illegal immigration We Have a Problem – namely, how to prevent it without adopting too obviously barbarous measures – because that was the line among megalopolitan intellectuals, raised to believe that trade unions and progressiveness are one. Instead he argued that Mexicans who come to America to better themselves, even if they hurt some workers with American passports, have equal claim to our ethical concern as people born north of the Rio Grande. To the audience at Princeton it was a startling idea, that the egalitarian ethic should extend to the wretchedly poor across the border. The shock in those liberal halls of intellectual power was palpable. People were embarrassed that someone had spoken against nationalism in ethics. It was evident that stories and metaphors about immigration, which spoke of good unions undermined by foreign scabs, were largely unexamined.

Talk of America's problem with foreign competition entails a bitter nationalism. The nationalistic, game-playing (and war-mongering) stories can fit with any sort of economics. Linked with socialism, they become national socialism, the better to protect the fatherland, or socialism in one country, the better to protect the mother-land. Linked with *laissez-faire*, they become imperialism, the better to protect United Fruit. As Smith said in 1776, 'A great empire has been established for the sole purpose of raising up a nation of customers who should be obliged to buy from the shops of our different producers'.[15] None of these can be the intent of Thurow and the anti-immigrationists and the other enthusiasts for protection and industrial planning. All the more reason to examine soberly their metaphors and stories.

The Productivity Problem in recent American history is not a figment. Americans are for instance alarmingly badly educated, considering their incomes (for which we professors, incidentally, need to take some blame). Maybe such embarrassment is to be expected out of the great experiment of getting along without an aristocracy. Tocqueville thought so, and he was often right. But in any case productivity has nothing to do with international competitiveness and the balance of payments. As your local economist will be glad to make clear, the pattern of trade depends on comparative advantage, not absolute advantage. That Michael Jordan can do everything with a basketball does not suggest a policy of having the rest of his team sit down. That some country – say fabled America of yore, 'dominant' in world manufacturing – can do both agriculture and manufacturing better than anyone else does not suggest a policy of making it do everything and import nothing. The overall level of productivity has no effect on America's trade balance. None. And the trade balance is not a measure of excellence. None. The two have nothing to do with each other. We could achieve an enormous and positive trade balance tomorrow with no pursuit of excellence by forbidding imports. Americans want to trade with Tatsuro, and it makes them better off to do so: that is all.

The idea is not to 'compete,' whatever that might mean in thrillingly collective policies, but to become skilled and hard-working and therefore rich. Why *foreign* trade should be especially important to the matter is obscure, though speaking against the outlanders is a common topic. The American economy, it happens, has been largely self-sufficient since its beginning, which is no surprise, since it stretches over half a continent. Lester Thurow pooh-poohs as not wealth-producing the 'taking in of one's own washing,' that is, trading with ourselves. But that is what Americans mainly do and always have done, with good results, thank you very much. The 'lost jobs,' to repeat, are mainly lost to *domestic* competition.

Like the failed war on poverty and the soon-to-fail war on drugs and the other attempts to arouse 'us' to face 'our' problems, the national challenge to engage in sporting and more bellicose competition with foreigners is snake oil. If it frightens Americans into investing more in bridges and education maybe it will do some good, by inadvertence. But the danger is using inapt and uncriticized stories and metaphors to rouse us from our slumber. The apter metaphors of economics say this: we do not need to be Number One in order to be happy and prosperous; we do not need to crush the Japanese to keep our self-respect.

So the ethics and policy of economic stories comes round to snake oil again. Eric Hoffer, the San Francisco dock worker and sage, asserted in one of his last books that 'The harm done by self-appointed experts in human affairs is usually a product of a priori logic ... the logic of events may draw from man's actions consequences which a priori logic cannot foresee'.[16] The distinction Hoffer had in mind is not between logic in the strict sense and events in the strict sense. He was no symbolic logician or runner of controlled experiments. He meant the distinction between metaphors and stories. The a priori logic is the extrapolated metaphor, such as the Third World or America's economic game. What we need from our experts is less pretended omniscience and more real wisdom, wisdom to tell the stories testing metaphors and to frame the metaphors that test the stories.

Reunifying some pieces of the conversation of humankind is best tried with hard cases. Economics is a hard case, wrapped in its prideful self-image as Social Physics. The neighbors of economics hate its arrogance, as the neighbors of physics do. If even economics can be shown to be fictional and poetical and historical its story will become better. Its experts will stop terrorizing the neighborhood and peddling snake oil. Technically speaking the economist's story will become, as it should, a useful comedy comprising words of wit, amused tolerance for human folly, stock characters colliding at last in the third act, and, most characteristic of the genre, a universe in equilibrium and a happy ending.

Notes

1.   D. N. McCloskey, *The Applied Theory of Price* (Macmillan, 1985), p. 345.
2.   See Susan M. Phillips and Richard Zecher, *The SEC and the Public Interest* (MIT Press, 1981).
3.   Peter Bauer, *Reality and Rhetoric* (Harvard University Press, 1984).
4.   *Ibid.*, p. 5.
5.   Mancur Olson, 'Diseconomies of Scale and Development', *Cato Journal*, 7 (Spring/Summer, 1987): 77–98.
6.   Lester Thurow, *The Zero-Sum Solution: Building a World-Class American Economy* (Simon & Schuster, 1985).
7.   *Ibid.*, p. 59.
8.   *Ibid.*, p. 107.
9.   *Ibid.*, p. 105.
10.   *Ibid.*, p. 48.
11.   *Ibid.*, p. 49.
12.   Adam Smith, *An Inquiry into the Nature and Causes of the Wealth of Nations*, ed. E. Cannan (University of Chicago Press, 1976 [1776]), p. 179.
13.   Thurow, *The Zero-Sum Solution*, pp. 100–1.
14.   D. N. McCloskey, *Enterprise and Trade in Victorian Britain* (Allen & Unwin, 1981), chap. 9.
15.   Smith, *Wealth of Nations*, vol. 2, p. 180.
16.   Eric Hoffer, *Before the Sabbath* (Harper & Row, 1979), p. 26, 28.

8 What Do Economists Know?*

Thomas C. Schelling

The title of my talk today was stimulated by a conversation I had forty years ago with Peter Bauer, the distinguished Cambridge University economist. I arrived early at a dinner for him, and before other guests arrived he proclaimed, provocatively, that the number of things that economists knew that were true, important, and not obvious, was no more than the fingers on one hand. I waited to hear what the four or five things were that were true, important, and not obvious, but other guests arrived, the conversation was interrupted, and I was left forever in suspense.

I reflected on the question from time to time. I couldn't be sure whether he meant there were only five things altogether that together we know, or there are many important things known but no *one* among us knows more than five of them. So my program was just to take inventory of how many things I knew in economics that were true, important, and not obvious, and to see whether they added up to five.

Of course, to say that I know five things is to imply that they must be true: I can't be said to know them if they are false. But I could believe them wrongly to be true. Peter Bauer may have meant that there are many more things that economists think they know – they just aren't true. Believing something makes it true to me but not to somebody of a more skeptical persuasion.

* Commencement address to the Department of Economics, University of California, Berkeley, CA, May 20, 1994. Published in *The American Economist*, 39 (Spring 1995), 20–2.

119

This excursion on truth is not just a play on words: some important things are true in a different way from the way some other important things are true. Similarly some things are obvious in a different way from other things; in fact some things are believed true precisely because they become obvious. I say 'become obvious' because my candidates for Peter Bauer's collection all have the characteristic that, while at first glance they are paradoxical, once understood they are seen as incapable of being false.

These are what are sometimes called accounting identities. When I was an undergraduate they were often disparaged as 'mere identities'. They were unfalsifiable statements and did not count as scientific truths. They were said to be true by definition.

Actually the truth of all scientific propositions depends on careful definition; but the truth of the so-called identities depends *only* on careful definition. They are not merely definitions; if they were, they would be obvious. But they can be derived from definitions if the definitions are carefully made consistent.

The simplest possible identity – it sounds obvious when I say it – is that in any sales transaction the value of the item sold equals the value of the item purchased. The need for careful definition arises even here: if there is a sales tax we have to treat it as either received by the seller or as a side payment to the tax authorities. That even this simple identity is not always obvious was apparent a few weeks ago when values on the stock exchanges dropped almost ten percent. I heard several intelligent-sounding conversations on national public radio about where all the money was going. People obviously were anxiously liquidating their portfolios and it seemed important to know what they were doing with the proceeds.

What apparently wasn't quite obvious was that no money was leaving the stock market. No money could leave the stock market. No one can sell a share of stock without a buyer: taxes and brokers' fees aside, for every dollar liquidated there has to be a dollar invested. Individuals, yes, were taking money out of stocks; but all investors together could not. Where the liquidated money was going might be interesting; but then equally interesting was a question not asked: where is all the money coming from? Together they had to cancel out. We can't all get rid of our Canadian quarters by passing them along at the first opportunity.

The national-income accounts contain a number of important identities. What they are is quadruple-entry consolidated income statements. Double-entry bookkeeping is for a single individual: but with every sale of goods or services there are two entries for the seller, two for the buyer. These accounts help us to understand the futility of efforts to get consumers to save more by spending less. The United States has a private savings rate lower than it used to be, lower than other industrial states. We citizens don't accomplish enough saving to promote faster improvements in productivity. It is seriously proposed that if we didn't use our credit cards to buy so many needless consumer goods we could have a more respectable rate of saving.

What apparently is not obvious is that the only way private citizens can accumulate savings is to consume less than their incomes, that is, to earn more than they spend on consumption. But there is no way they can all earn more than they consume except by producing equivalent goods that are not consumed. Somebody has to buy those goods. They can be domestic investment, exports, or government purchases; if those do not increase, it is impossible for private saving to increase. I can save another $10 by going without a haircut; but my barber's income goes down by $10, and his savings too, unless he cuts his own spending, in which case he passes along the loss in a chain reaction that offsets my $10 saving.

Because you graduates have learned this truth it may seem obvious; but it wasn't obvious to you until you learned it, it isn't obvious to most people out there, and it wasn't obvious to economists when I entered Berkeley.

There are other important accounting truths. Most bankers understand their own balance sheets well; what most bankers don't know is that whenever they make a loan they increase the money supply. They don't know it because, as they see it, they only lend money that already exists, money in the bank's reserves. What they don't see is that the reserves still exist – they have simply migrated to other banks – while the customer's money also still exists; it, too, has migrated.

Most of the nonobvious accounting propositions are true only in the aggregate, not true for the individual. They do not correspond to the experience of the banker who lends only money that he has in reserve, or the consumer who forgoes the haircut. But they hold in the same way that the laws of conservation do – conservation of energy, mass, or momentum. If we launch a squash court into orbit, the momentum of its center of gravity will be undisturbed by the game being played inside. In the physical sciences many of these accounting identities are dignified with the title, 'law'; and like the identities in economics they were not obvious without an intellectual struggle. The conservation of momentum – that a moving object will continue moving at the same speed and in the same direction forever until resisted, pushed, deflected, or subjected to friction – has become obvious, but because it couldn't be observed anywhere in the universe until space flight became possible, its becoming obvious required laboratory experiment and intellectual struggle.

It is sometimes said, in textbooks and in learned volumes, that these accounting statements, being unfalsifiable, do not count as science. I don't care. The question is whether they tell you something important you didn't know. The history of our discipline demonstrates that they are not obvious. Disparaging them as 'mere identities' at least testifies to their truth. They are the foundation of any macroeconomics. They have their counterparts in physics, chemistry, biology, genetics, and our sister discipline, demography. They are sometimes known as 'budgets'; there is the earth's energy budget, its carbon budget, its water budget, even budgets for nondegradable substances like DDT.

There are many more than five important accounting identities in economics that are not obvious; I could have mentioned the balance of payments, or the input-output matrix. As to their importance, where I would draw the line – at five or ten – I don't know. Some of them were surely unknown to Peter Bauer; the carbon budget was unrecognized when I had dinner with him.

So if I am allowed five candidates, they are all accounting identities. I cannot hope to have persuaded you in twenty minutes, but I hope I have sensitized you to be on watch for them, to respect and appreciate them, and not to be afraid of counting them among the things you know that are true and important and were not obvious before you studied economics, even though they do not count as empirically grounded, potentially falsifiable, scientific hypotheses.

I am tempted to close these remarks with a small investigation into what it is that economists know that are important, not obvious, and *not* true. Actually, what I have in mind is propositions or principles that are true but that unintentionally, the way they are formulated, appear to deny something that is also true, raising the question: which deserves the more emphasis, the truth contained in the proposition, or the truth the proposition appears to deny?

I have a candidate. It has become fashionable in the last two decades, not only among economists but among those who like to quote economists, to advert to an incontestable, absolute truth colloquially expressed as: there is no free lunch.

The truth that I think this assertion is intended to communicate is that resources are always scarce, there are competing ends and competing beneficiaries, redistributing in someone's favor is at someone's expense and there is no alchemy in economics: you can recycle, but it is hard to find the equivalent of a nuclear breeder reactor that produces, in burning fuel, more fuel than it burns.

Maybe it's because of where I've been in economics, but I prefer the alternative truth, that there are free lunches all over just waiting to be discovered or created. What I have in mind is what we technically call Pareto improvements, or the gains from trade. There are non-zero sum games that permeate the economy that have settled into, or have been forced into, inefficient equilibria.

There are not just free lunches but banquets awaiting the former socialist countries that can institute enforceable contract, copyrights, and patents, or eliminate rent-free housing and energy subsidies. How the lunches get distributed matters; but the lunches are there.

Those of you who move into the economics profession, in government, academia, or in business, will spend much of your time exploring for opportunities to eliminate constraints on mutually beneficial trading, to overcome market failures and to create markets where they are needed, to identify removable deadweight losses, and to promote integrative bargaining.

This is what we do in economics. Technological innovation can push out the production frontier; it is economists who help to find where we are deep inside that frontier, diagnose what keeps us from the frontier, and propose institutional changes to bring us closer to the frontier. To those of you who become professional economists I urge you: get out there and help find those free lunches.

9 Economists and the Correction of Error*

Israel M. Kirzner

The dust jacket on this book displays a photograph of its distinguished author, our most recent Nobel laureate in economics, standing behind an impressively ornate pulpit, grasping the lectern firmly with both hands, with a glint in his eye suggesting an imminent outpouring of fire-and-brimstone rhetoric. On more careful examination of this arresting picture, one observes that the vestments worn by the author are academic rather than ecclesiastical, leading one, in the light of the book's title, to guess that the sermon would hold out the threat of economic, rather than spiritual, perdition. But a glance through the book quickly shows that nothing could be further from the truth. George Stigler has only one sermon to preach in this volume, and that is to denounce the fatuity and futility of economic preaching itself.

Now, this sermon will, for most economists and laymen alike, appear shocking. And, indeed, many pages in this new collection of Professor Stigler's papers – characteristically replete with sparkling wit, sardonic wisdom, and the fruits of extensive and meticulous scholarship – are dedicated to the task of shattering a pleasing self-image that most economists enjoy. In this self-image, society is seen as all too frequently pursuing deplorably mistaken policies – mistaken, that is, in being likely to generate results that society prefers less than other outcomes. The

* A review essay on George J. Stigler, *The Economist as Preacher and Other Essays* (Chicago: University of Chicago Press, 1982). Originally published with the title, 'Does Anyone Listen to Economists?', *Inquiry: A Libertarian Review*, April 1983, pp. 38–40.

source of these mistakes is seen as arising out of regrettably widespread ignorance of economics truths. The economist is, therefore, seen as being able, by virtue of his possession of superior economic wisdom, to reveal to society what policies are in fact the correct ones. The provision of such policy recommendations, and the exhortations to avoid economic error, are what Stigler identifies as the *preaching* in which economists engage.

Like other preachers, economists tend to enjoy their privileged position in the pulpit, the prestige they derive from public awareness of this privileged position, and the material rewards associated with such privilege and prestige. What Stigler wishes to do in this book is to take the fun (and presumably the profit) out of economic preaching. What I shall argue in this review is that, in engaging in this sermonizing against economic sermons, Stigler is, besides being an iconoclastic spoilsport or engaging gadfly, consistently pursuing one particular, unfortunate, view of the scope of economics to its predictably bizarre conclusion.

Two stages may be discerned in the development of Stigler's argument. In Chapter 5 (a paper originally published in 1976) Stigler asks, 'Do Economists Matter?' That is, are economists listened to? Can any improvements in societal well-being be credited to the benign teachings of economists? His strongly negative answer was advanced in the form of a bald thesis: 'Economists exert a minor and scarcely detectable influence on the societies in which they live.' Let us call this the First Stigler Thesis. Notice that this first thesis merely says that while it *might* indeed be wise and useful for societies to pay heed to the preachings of economists, the sad truth happens to be that they pay no such heed. (Or, more precisely, they pay heed only to those preachings they themselves independently favor, and which they have in fact themselves solicited to be preached.) So that, disconcerting though it may be for economists to hear that nobody really listens to them, they can at least continue to feel comforted in the warm conviction that their unsolicited preachings, even if ignored or spurned, nonetheless really might be good for the economic soul of society.

It is this residual semblance of a satisfying self-image for the economist that Stigler seeks to explode in the title essay (Chapter 1) and in the two following chapters (the three essays having been delivered as lectures in 1980). Stigler's Second Thesis asserts in effect that economists have nothing useful to tell society. When economists claim to perceive mistaken economic policies, it is in fact the economists who are likely to be the mistaken ones. Societies generally do not need any policy advice from economists; they generally know where their interests lie, and how to pursue these interests. The reason why economists exercise negligible influence on society through their preaching is, of course, simply because these preachings are (unless solicited by society in the first place) in fact valueless for society; societies sense this and, therefore, quite properly ignore these high-minded but useless sermons. With Stigler's Second Thesis, all that is left for economists is to talk professionally to themselves – an occupation that Stigler indeed believes to be honorable and worthwhile (and anyway one that, in his opinion, in fact makes up the bulk of professional activity) but nonetheless one unlikely, it would appear, to be judged so important as to warrant the volume of resources that society allocates for the care and feeding of its economists.

These two theses are undoubtedly intended by their author to disturb his fellow economists. The disturbing quality of Stigler's Theses derives, it should be pointed out, in large measure from his claim that these challenges to the self-image of economists *are grounded solidly in the most fundamental teachings of economics itself.* Consider the First Thesis. There are few more central theorems in economics than that which demonstrates a tendency for production in market economies to be directed by the interests and preferences of consumers. Well, then, Stigler points out, the theorem ought to apply also to 'the production of the words and ideas of intellectuals'. That is, the ideas produced by economists are, according to this central economic theorem, directed by consumers rather than vice versa. So that it is not the teachings of economists which influence the behavior of policy makers, but rather the interests and preferences of members of and groups in society that determine the ideas taught by economists. Stigler is careful not to claim that economics teaches that economists necessarily engage in intellectual prostitution (although he is equally careful not to claim that intellectuals possess more courage or integrity than others). He merely claims that the market will encourage the production of those sermons it prefers to hear, with the consequence that economists able sincerely to produce those ideas will find a market for their books and lectures, while those unable sincerely to do so will find no market for their wares and will presumably turn to teaching or to other innocent pursuits.

Or, again, consider what we have called Stigler's Second Thesis, the denial of the idea that societies might be likely, unless they pay heed to the preachings of economists, to pursue mistaken policies. Stigler links this thesis with premises that he considers to be very basic to economics. It is, Stigler declares, most unsatisfactory for a discipline that assumes man to be a reasonably efficient utility-maximizer to treat public policy in economic affairs 'as a curious mixture of benevolent public interest and unintentional blunders'. In fact, Stigler maintains, 'a theory that says that a large set of persistent policies are mistaken is profoundly anti-intellectual unless it is joined to a theory of mistakes'. Because economics, in Stigler's view, emphatically lacks such a theory of mistakes, it seems to point unavoidably toward Stigler's Second Thesis. The premises upon which economists build their science should, it appears, lead them to conclude that their own social usefulness in recommending policy is close to nil.

As witty paradoxes deftly aimed at the pomposity of much economic preaching, Stigler's theses can be cheerfully accepted; as general propositions seriously advanced, however, Stigler's bizarre conclusions can and should be firmly disputed. The affront to common sense that these

Stiglerian Theses so provocatively offer, arises, in my view, not from consistent application of sound economic principles, but from a highly unfortunate approach to economic theorizing that Stigler has endorsed. Sound economic principles do not lead ineluctably to the Stiglerian conclusions; naughtily attractive though this claim might be, it is just not the case that economics teaches the worthlessness of economic policy advice.

The issue revolves, of course, around the role of *error* and, more particularly, of the *correction* of error, in economic analysis. For a long time much of modern economic theory depended (and in some circles still seems to depend) on the assumption that decision makers correctly know the full facts relevant to their choices. No decision maker ever made a mistake. In fact, the assumption that all decisions are made correctly tended to be carried to the point where (since a decision is correct only if it correctly anticipates the relevant decisions of others) economic analysis was conducted by taking it for granted that *all* decisions of *all* market participants have somehow been *prereconciled* (to permit them all to be made correctly).

There is no doubt that for many important analytical purposes this way of seeing the world as being always close to errorless equilibrium was extremely helpful. For many purposes the ability to abstract from error and from processes of error-correction permitted economists to arrive at simple and reasonably correct understandings of economic phenomena. But, as we witness in the development of Stigler's position, the assumption that error is absent from economic analysis, useful though this assumption has been for so many purposes, has carried with it a rather heavy price. It is one thing to treat error as nonexistent for purposes where its presence is relatively unimportant; it is quite another thing to imagine away error in contexts where the phenomena that one would explain by error *can in fact only be understood by reference to error and to the processes of error-correction*. Yet this is exactly what Stigler appears to have done.

Now, this accusation must be made with some care. It is certainly not correct to accuse Stigler of having no place in his economics for imperfect knowledge, and for the processes of the enhancement of such knowledge. In fact, Professor Stigler has himself been a pioneer in the development of the branch of economic analysis that deals with the theory of *search for superior information*. But valuable though the economic theory of search unquestionably is, it must be pointed out that it does not attempt to grapple with what, in terms of our present discussion, we have referred to as *error*. It is certainly possible (as is done in the economic theory of search) to include, among the decisions being taken by market participants, decisions to deliberately undertake costly programs of information-search. But the point is that, for the theory of search, these decisions are *themselves*, in effect, made without possibility of error. That is, each potential searcher correctly knows, in effect, how much it will cost to gain additional information and how valuable such additional information is likely to be. What one decides not to learn may indeed represent an imperfection in knowledge, but it represents a *correctly calculated* imperfection. To have learned *more* would, in the light of relevant search costs, have been an error. So it remains an accurate commentary on Stiglerian economics (and in fact this has been emphasized by Stigler himself) that it simply has no place for true error. My contention is that for an understanding of certain economic phenomena an appreciation of the role of error and of its correction is crucially important. For Stiglerian economics such phenomena must necessarily be blocked out of the economist's picture of the world. It is Stigler's perverse consistency in this regard that has led him to his odd conclusions regarding the possibility of valuable economic policy advice.

The truth is that the social marvel that is constituted by the market economy arises not out of any unexplained prereconciliation of errorless decision makers, but from a systematic, entrepreneurial 'discovery procedure' (to use Hayek's phrase). In this entrepreneurial process, sheer error and its discovery *are of the essence.* There is absolutely no mystery in the prevalence of economic policy error; there is absolutely no need to presume that we live at all times in the best of all possible worlds; there is absolutely no reason to doubt that society could benefit by attention to such sound economic advice (suggested by economic analysis) as that supporting the enhancement of freedom for entrepreneurial competition, and the elimination of economic privilege. No doubt there is much spurious economic advice offered (and paid for); no doubt there is much unnecessary and wrong-headed preaching engaged in by economists; but the a priori declaration that all economic sermons are valueless is simply without foundation.

This slim volume contains many wise and erudite explorations in the sociology and history of economics. In all these explorations Stigler shows himself the master historian of ideas, with a keen eye for the intellectual foibles of economists in all generations. Many of these essays in the history of economic thought will remain of permanent worth to the specialist. But the importance of this book will be gauged, in the last analysis, by its impact upon the thinking of the educated laymen (to whom so much of it, including its intriguing dust jacket, is clearly addressed). It will be unfortunate indeed if this fascinating volume succeeds in popularizing the altogether unfounded notion that greater and more widespread economic understanding can make no contribution to the betterment of the human condition.

10 On Being an Economist*

Friedrich A. Hayek

It is reported of the greatest economist whom I have personally known that he used to say that if he had seven sons they should all study economics. If this was meant to suggest the magnitude of the task economists have to solve, this heroic resolution cannot be highly enough commended. If it was meant to suggest that the study of economics is a sure path to personal happiness, I am afraid I have no such cheerful message for you. And it may be that Carl Menger himself later changed his views: when at last, at the age of sixty-two, he produced one son, this son did not become an economist, though the father lived to see him become a promising mathematician.

There is at least one kind of happiness which the pursuit of most sciences promises but which is almost wholly denied to the economist. The progress of the natural sciences often leads to unbounded confidence in the future prospects of the human race, and provides the natural scientist with the certainty that any important contribution to knowledge which he makes will be used to improve the lot of men. The economist's lot, however, is to study a field in which, almost more than any other, human folly displays itself. The scientist has no doubt that the world is moving on to better and finer things, that the progress he makes today will tomorrow be recognized and

* An address delivered to the Students' Union of the London School of Economics, February 23, 1944. First published in *The Trend of Economic Thinking: Essays on Political Economists and Economic History* (Volume III of *The Collected Works of F. A. Hayek*), edited by W. W. Bartley III and Stephen Kresge (Chicago: University of Chicago Press, 1991), pp. 35–48.

used. There is a glamour about the natural sciences which expresses itself in the spirit and the atmosphere in which it is pursued and received, in the prizes that wait for the successful as in the satisfaction it can offer to most. What I want to say to you tonight is a warning that, if you want any of this, if to sustain you in the toil which the prolonged pursuit of any subject requires, you want these clear signs of success, you had better leave economics and turn to one of the more fortunate other sciences. Not only are there no glittering prizes, no Nobel prizes and – I should have said till recently – no fortunes and no peerages,[1] for the economist. But even to look for them, to aim at praise or public recognition, is almost certain to spoil your intellectual honesty in this field. The dangers to the economist from any too strong desire to win public approval, and the reasons why I think it indeed fortunate that there are only few marks of distinction to corrupt him, I shall discuss later. But before that I want to consider the more serious cause for sorrow to the economist, the fact that he cannot trust that the progress of his knowledge will necessarily be followed by a more intelligent handling of social affairs, or even that we shall advance in this field at all and there will not be retrograde movements. The economist knows that a single error in his field may do more harm than almost all the sciences taken together can do good – even more, that a mistake in the choice of a social order, quite apart from the immediate effect, may profoundly affect the prospects for generations. Even if he believes that he is himself in possession of full truth – which he believes less the older he grows – he cannot be sure that it will be used. And he cannot even be sure that his activities will not produce, because they are mishandled by others, the opposite of what he was aiming at.

I shall not argue that the economist has no influence. On the contrary, I agree with Lord Keynes that 'the ideas of economists and political philosophers, both when they are right and when they are wrong, are more powerful than is commonly understood. Indeed the world is ruled by little else'.[2] The only qualification I want to add, and with which Lord Keynes would probably agree, is that economists have this great influence only in the long run and only indirectly, and that when their ideas begin to have effect, they have usually changed their form to such an extent that their fathers can scarcely recognize them.

This is closely connected with the fact, inevitable I believe in a democracy, that those who have to apply economic theory are laymen, not really trained as economists. In this economics differs from other disciplines. We do not, as the other sciences do, train practitioners who are called in when an economic problem arises – or they can at most be called in as advisers while the actual decisions must be left to the statesman and the general public. However attractive the ideal of a government by experts may have appeared in the past – it even induced a radical liberal like John Stuart Mill to state that:

of all governments, ancient and modern, the one by which this excellence [i.e., that political questions are decided 'by the deliberately formed opinion of a comparatively few, specially educated for the task'] is possessed in the most eminent degree is the government of Prussia – a most powerfully and skilfully organised aristocracy of all the most highly educated men in the kingdom.[3]

We know now where this leads. And we prefer, I think rightly, an imperfect government by democratic methods to a real government by experts.

However, this has consequences of which economists more than others ought to be aware. We can never be sure what our suggestions will produce and whether our best meant efforts may not result in something very different from what we wish. It is, in fact, quite conceivable that advance in social knowledge may produce a retrogression in social policy, and this has indeed happened more than once. I will give you only one example. About seventy years ago economists began seriously to urge certain exceptions to the free-trade argument then almost universally accepted. I am not concerned here whether they were right or wrong. The point I want to make is merely that when after the usual interval of a generation or so their ideas began to take effect they produced a state of affairs which, I believe, even the most extreme protectionists would agree to be greatly inferior to the conditions of near free trade they had attacked. It may be true that some little protection, or some little flexibility in exchange rates, judiciously administered, may be better than free trade or the gold standard. I don't believe it, but it may be true. But this does not exclude that the advocacy of these modifications may have most regrettable effects. The attack against the principle, or perhaps half-truth, of the free-trade doctrine has certainly had the effect that the public forgot even a great deal of the elementary economics it had learnt, and became once more ready to assent to absurdities which seventy years ago it would have laughed out of court.

I have just referred to the interval of a generation or so which usually elapses before a new opinion becomes a political force. This phenomenon will be familiar to the readers of Dicey's *Law and Opinion*,[4] and I could add many further instances to those given there. But it is perhaps specially necessary to remind you of it, because the unique rapidity with which, in our own time, the teaching of Lord Keynes has penetrated into public consciousness may a little mislead you about what is the more regular course of things. I shall presently have to suggest an explanation of this exceptional case.

Another point to which I have indirectly referred already, but on which I must dwell a little, is the fact that in our field no knowledge can be regarded as established once and for all, and that, in fact, knowledge once gained and spread is often not disproved, but simply lost and forgotten. The elements of the free-trade argument, at one time nearly understood by every educated man, are a case in point. The reason why in our field knowledge can be so lost is, of course, that it is never established by experiment, but can be acquired only by following a rather difficult process of reasoning. And people will believe a thing if you just tell them 'it has been shown by experiment' – although they may understand nothing about it – they will not accept in the same manner an argument, even though that argument may have convinced everybody who has understood it. The result is that in economics you can never establish a truth once and for all but have always to convince every generation anew – and that you may find much more difficult when things appear to yourself no longer so simple as they once did.

I cannot attempt here more than to touch upon the inexhaustible subject of *Economists and the Public*, a subject on which Professor H. Hutt of Capetown has written a thoughtful book, which contains many wise things and some not so wise – and which I strongly recommend to your attention. There are very interesting points in this connexion, which have considerable bearing on our professional position as economists, such as the special difficulty, in our field, of distinguishing between the expert and the quack – and the equally important fact of the traditional unpopularity of the economists. You probably all know the remark of Walter Bagehot that the public has never yet been sorry to hear of the death of an economist. In fact, the dislike for most of the teaching of the economists in the past has built up a picture of the economist as a sort of monster devouring children. There is little to justify it in the facts. One of the great liberal politicians of the early nineteenth century (Sir James Mackintosh) has said that 'he had known Smith slightly, Ricardo well and Malthus intimately and found them about the best men he had known'. I can to some extent confirm this. As you perhaps know I have amused myself at times by digging into the history of economics, and during the past twenty-five years I have had the opportunity to know not only a good many economists of this and the past generation but also to compare them with scholars in other fields. And I must say I have found them on the whole a surprisingly nice, sensitive and sane lot of people, less crotchety and mad than other scientists. Yet they still enjoy a reputation worse than almost any other profession and are imagined to be particularly hard, prejudiced, and devoid of feeling. And it was, and still is, the most eminent of economists in an academic sense, towards whom these reproaches were most frequently directed, while nothing is easier than for a crank to acquire the reputation of being a friend of the people. Things are in this respect still very much the same as they were in Adam Smith's time, and what he said about the relation of an MP to monopolies applies very much to the relation of the economist to the practical 'interests' – and not only the capitalist interests: 'The member of parliament', you will find it said in the *Wealth of Nations*,[5]

> who supports every proposal for strengthening this monopoly (of house manufacturers), is sure to acquire not only the reputation of understanding trade, but great popularity and influence with an order of men whose number and wealth render them of great importance. If he opposes them, on the contrary, and still more if he has authority enough to thwart them, neither the most acknowledged probity, nor the highest rank, nor the greatest public services, can protect him from the most infamous abuse and detraction, from personal insults, nor sometimes real danger, arising from the insolent outrage of furious and disappointed monopolists.

Before I pursue this subject of the effect of public opinion and political bias on the work of the economist I must for a moment pause to consider the various reasons and purposes which make us study economics. It is probably still true of most of us – and in this, too, economics differs from most other subjects – that we did not turn to economics for the fascination of the subject as such. Whatever may guide us later, few do – or at least did in my time – turn to economics for that reason simply because we usually don't quite know what economics is. Indeed I remember that when I first borrowed during the last war from a fellow officer a textbook on economics[6] I was strongly repelled by the dreariness of what I found, and my social enthusiasm was hardly sufficient to make me plod through the tome in which I hoped to find – and needless to say, did not find – the answer to the burning problem of how to build a juster society for which I really cared. But while the motives which have led most of us – and I hope most of you – to the study of economics are highly commendable, they are not very conducive to real advance of insight. The fact which we must face is that nearly all of us come to the study of economics with very strong views on subjects which we do not understand. And even if we make a show of being detached and ready to learn, I am afraid it is almost always with a mental reservation, with an inward determination to prove that our instincts were right and that nothing we learn can change our basic convictions. Though I am verging dangerously on preaching, let me nevertheless implore you to make a determined effort to achieve that intellectual humility which alone helps one to learn. Nothing is more pernicious to intellectual honesty than pride in not having changed one's opinions – particularly if, as is usually the case in our field, these are opinions which in the circles in which we move are regarded as 'progressive' or 'advanced' or just modern. You will soon enough discover that what you regard as specially advanced opinions are just the opinions dominant in your particular generation and that it requires much greater strength and independence of mind to take a critical view of what you have been taught to be progressive than merely to accept them.

Back to my main topic. The great majority of you necessarily study the social sciences not with the intention of going on to study them for the rest of your lives, but with a view to a job in which in the near future you can use your knowledge. You will then be entirely concerned with what is practical and will have to take the dominant ideals and ideas of your time for granted. Though in the long run it may be the economist who creates these ruling ideas, what he can do in practice is determined by the ideas created by his fathers or grandfathers. Does that mean that in academic study, too, we ought to be concerned with the immediately practical, take the current of ideas for granted, and prepare ourselves for the particular job we shall probably be called upon to perform? Now I do not believe that the universities can do this or that they would perform their proper function if they attempted to do it. I do not think that in the social sciences the universities could give an effective 'professional training' or that persons so trained would be of much use except for subordinate jobs. The practical aspects of a particular job are much better learnt on the job – and that is even true of many of the more general concrete aspects of the society in which we live. What you need, if through that inevitable apprenticeship you hope ultimately to rise to more responsible positions, is a capacity to interpret the detail with which you will be concerned and to see through the catchwords and phrases which govern everyday life. Does the study of the social sciences as it is now pursued provide this education, or how can it be made to do so?

This raises immediately the vexed problem of specialization versus a general and all-round education, much more acute and difficult in the social sciences than anywhere else. Let me meet a common misunderstanding: it is often argued that in social life everything hangs so closely together that society can only be studied 'as a whole'. If that were really the case it would mean that it could not be studied at all. Nobody is capable of really understanding all aspects of society, and so far as advancement of knowledge is concerned specialization is in the social sciences as necessary as anywhere, and becomes daily more necessary. But in another sense the contention that exclusive knowledge of a single sector of the social sciences is of little use is perfectly true. While you may be a very useful member of society if you are a competent chemist or biologist but know nothing else, you will not be a useful member of society if you know only economics or political science and nothing else. You cannot successfully use your technical knowledge unless you are a fairly educated person, and, in particular, have some knowledge of the whole field of the social sciences as well as some knowledge of history and philosophy. Of course real competence in some particular field comes first. Unless you really know your economics or whatever your special field is, you will be simply a fraud. But if you know only economics and nothing else, you will be a bane to mankind, good, perhaps, for writing articles for other economists to read, but for nothing else. If you have only three years[7] this double task of acquiring technical competence in a narrow field plus a general education is a formidable task. But you will find it will for long be the only opportunity you have to collect a great deal of varied knowledge whose meaning and significance you will recognize only later. And if you mean to make the academic study of one of the subjects your life-work, it is even more important that during your undergraduate years you let your interests range rather widely. Any successful original work on one of the social sciences requires now many years of exacting and exclusive attention to a narrow field, and it will be only after ten or fifteen years in which by such work you have become entitled to regard yourself as a creative economist that you once again emerge as a man who can look at things in a wider perspective and can broaden out beyond your narrow specialism. It is in the years before you have become specialists, before you have tied yourself to a particular field or a particular purpose, that you must acquire what general education you will have to guide you in the most active and productive part of your life.

What I want to plead for here is that in this you should let yourself be guided not by any fixed purpose but mainly by intellectual curiosity and a spirit of exploration. Apart from what you need for examination purposes there is no definite field of knowledge which you can hope to have 'covered' by the time you complete your course. And you will derive infinitely more profit if you allow yourself to follow up problems which at the moment interest you, or interest yourself in questions which you feel are definitely interesting, than if you make it a set purpose to master a definite subject. That you do enough of that the impending examinations see to. But no man or woman deserves to be at a university whose intellectual energy is completely absorbed by that except in the last months before the exams, in work for the exam. Unless you use the opportunities you now have in this respect you will never make the gain which I still regard as the greatest of all that the university can give: the discovery that to learn, to come to understand things, can be the greatest of human pleasures, and the only one that will never be exhausted.

I see I let myself again and again be drawn away from what I wanted to talk more about than anything, and as time is now getting short I must concentrate entirely on that one point. It is a point connected with the one I have just discussed – the way in which, not as beginners, but in our original work as economists, we guide and direct our interests. Should we aim at immediate usefulness, should we concern ourselves mainly with what is immediately practicable? Or should we pursue whatever intellectual difficulty we feel we might be able to solve, follow up problems where we see accepted views are defective or muddled and where, therefore, we can hope to effect some theoretical improvement, irrespective of whether we can now see what its practical significance will be or not? The question is, of course, closely connected with whether the economist should strive for immediate influence or whether the economist should be content to work in effect for a distant future in which he has little personal interest. This is, of course, a choice which only the academic economist, the 'don', has to make; but it is nevertheless of some importance.

When I stress the unpopular and unfashionable answer to these questions I do not, of course, mean to imply that these are really exclusive alternatives and that a sensible person will not aim at some judicious balance between the two. What I want to suggest is merely that the 'academic' attitude which I shall favor is being unduly disparaged at the moment and the dangers to full intellectual integrity and independence which the more 'practical' attitude involves are perhaps not fully enough recognized.

The reason why I think that too deliberate striving for immediate usefulness is so likely to corrupt the intellectual integrity of the economist is that immediate usefulness depends almost entirely on influence, and influence is gained most easily by concessions to popular prejudice and adherence to existing political groups. I seriously believe that any such striving for popularity (at least till you have very definitely settled your own convictions) is fatal to the economist and that above anything he must have the courage to be unpopular. Whatever his theoretical beliefs may be, when he has to deal with the proposals of laymen the chance is that in nine out of ten cases his answer will have to be that their various ends are incompatible and that they will have to choose between them and to sacrifice some ambitions which they cherish. This is an inevitable consequence of the type of problems with which he has to deal: problems which are well described by the lines of Schiller that

With ease by one another dwell the thoughts
But hard in space together clash the things.

The economist's task is precisely to detect such incompatibilities of thoughts before the clash of the things occurs, and the result is that he will always have the ungrateful task of pointing out the costs. That's what he is there for and it is a task from which he must never shirk, however unpopular and disliked it may make him. Whatever else you may think of the classical economists you must admit that they never feared being unpopular.

It is fashionable now to sneer at their 'non-conformist conscience' or 'self-castigating spirit' which found pleasure in recommending all sorts of self-denial. And perhaps at a time when to adhere to their doctrines was essential to respectability there really was not as much merit in their stern attitude as some of them might claim. But the pendulum has now so much swung in the opposite direction, the fashion is now so much to give the public what it wants rather than to warn it that it cannot have all, that it is worth remembering how much easier this is than to take the unpopular course. I think as economists we should at least always suspect ourselves if we find that we are on the popular side. It is so much easier to believe pleasant conclusions, or to trace doctrines which others like to believe, to concur in the views which are held by most people of good will, and not to disillusion enthusiasts, that the temptation to accept views which would not stand cold examination is sometimes almost irresistible.

It is the desire to gain influence in order to be able to do good which is one of the main sources of intellectual concessions by economist. I do not mean, and do not wish to argue, that the economist should entirely refrain from making value judgements or from speaking frankly on political questions. I do not believe that the former is possible or the latter desirable. But I think he ought to avoid committing himself to a party – or even devoting himself predominantly to some one good cause. That not only warps judgement – but the influence it gives him is almost certainly bought at the price of intellectual independence. Too much anxiety to get a particular thing done, or to keep one's influence over a particular group, is almost certain to be an obstacle to his saying many unpopular things he ought to say – and leads to his compromising with 'dominant views' which have to be accepted, and even accepting views which would not stand serious examination.

I trust you will forgive me if I seriously suggest that the danger of such intellectual corruption, of concession made to the desire of gaining influence, is today greater from what are known as the left or progressive parties than from those of the right. The forces of the right are usually neither intelligent enough to value the support of intellectual activities, nor have they the sort of prizes to offer which are likely to influence honest people. But the fact that, whatever may be true of the country as a whole, the 'intelligentsia' is predominantly left means that you are certain to have much greater influence, and therefore apparently chances to be useful, if you accept the sort of views which are generally regarded as 'progressive'. There are now, and probably always will be, any number of attractive jobs, such as various sorts of research or adult education, in which you will be welcomed if you hold the right kind of 'progressive' views, and will have a better chance of getting on various committees or commissions if you represent any known political programme than if you are known to go your own way. Never forget that the reputation of being 'progressive' adheres almost always to people or movements which have already half succeeded in converting people.[8]

There can be no question that in resisting the inclination to join in with some popular movement one deliberately excludes oneself from much that is pleasant, profitable and flattering. Yet I believe that in our field more than in any other this is really essential: if anyone, the economist must keep free not to believe things which it would be useful and pleasant to believe, must not allow himself to encourage wish-dreams in himself or others. I don't think the work of the politician and the true student of society are compatible. Indeed it seems to me that in order to be successful as a politician, to become a political leader, it is almost essential that you have no original ideas on social matters but just express what the majority feel. But I have perhaps said already more than enough about the external temptations and I want to say only a few more words about the internal ones, the seductive attraction exercised by the pleasantness of certain views. Here, too, there has recently been a great change of attitude. While the classical economists were perhaps a little too apt to feel 'that is too good to be true', I believe this attitude is still a safer one than the feeling that the conclusions of an argument are so desirable that they must be true.

I can illustrate this position only from my own experience and that will probably be different from yours. From all considerations other than the purely scientific one I have every reason to wish that I were able to believe that a planned socialist society can achieve what its advocates promise. If I could convince myself that they are right this would suddenly remove all the clouds which to me blacken all the prospects of the future. I should be free to share in the happy confidence of so many of my fellow men and to join with them in the work for a common end. As an economist such a situation would indeed have a double attraction. As I am again and again reminded by some socialist colleagues, our special knowledge would secure us a much more important position and I might rise to be a trusted leader instead of a hated obstructionist. You will probably say that of course it is only pride which, once I have staked my professional reputation on a certain view, now prevents me from seeing the truth. But it was not always so. And I have indeed been mainly thinking of the extremely painful process of disillusionment which led me to my present views.

You will probably not have the experience in the same connexion, but I am sure that, if you do not regard your economics just as a given instrument to achieve given ends, but as a continuous adventure in the search for truth, you will sooner or later have a similar experience in one connexion or another. It will be for you as well a choice between cherished and pleasant illusions on the one side and the ruthless pursuit of an argument which will lead you almost certainly into isolation and unpopularity and which you do not know where else it will lead. I believe this duty to face and think through unpleasant facts is the hardest task of the economist and the reason why, if he fulfils it, he must not look for public approval or sympathy for his efforts. If he does he will soon cease to be an economist and become a politician – a very honourable and useful calling, but a different one, and not one which gives the kind of satisfaction we expect when we embark on an intellectual pursuit. It is this choice about which I wanted to talk and of the necessity of which I mainly wanted to warn you. There are, as you will realize more and more, many self-denying ordinances which the economist must pass on himself if he wants to remain true to his vocation. But the most important of them seems to me that he must never directly aim at immediate success and public influence. I do not go as far as Professor Hutt in the book mentioned who wants the economists to submit to an almost monastic discipline in order to protect them from corruption. But I believe there is more truth in what he says than is commonly admitted. And I don't know that any economist will be happy in his profession till he has made the choice and, if he chooses the pursuit of light rather than of fruits, reconciles himself with these limitations.

If he is able to do so I believe he has a better chance in the long run to contribute to the improvement of our social problems than if he more directly strove for it. I am also convinced that if he has made the renunciation there is a great deal of real pleasure in his work, just as there would be if he had equally wholeheartedly devoted himself to any more tangible and definite goal. So far as I myself am concerned, at any rate, and in spite of what I have said, I have never really regretted that I became an economist, or really wished to change with anybody else.

But I have been long enough. It was not my intention when I started to preach a sermon, and if I have sometimes more than verged on it, you must forgive me. It was the first and I trust will be the last sermon I shall ever preach. And it has taken this form not because I am anxious to convert you to my point of view, but rather because I had to talk about questions which have deeply concerned me and where it has cost me considerable efforts to clear my own mind, and on which in consequence I feel strongly.

[Editor's Postscript: It is perhaps noteworthy that in the Preface to the Second Edition of his *Denationalisation of Money* (1978) Hayek wrote:

I ought, perhaps, also to add, what I have often had occasion to explain but may never have stated in writing, that I strongly feel that the chief task of the economic theorist or political philosopher should be to operate on public opinion to make politically possible what today may be politically impossible, and that in consequence the objection that my proposals are at present impracticable does not in the least deter me from developing them.]

Notes

1. [The reference is obviously to Keynes, who was created a Baron in 1942. – Ed. of Hayek's work.]
2. *The General Theory of Employment Interest and Money* (London: Macmillan, 1936), p. 383.
3. [John Stuart Mill, 'Rationale of Representation' [1835], in *Essays on Politics and Society* (Toronto: University of Toronto Press; London: Routledge & Kegan Paul, 1977), p. 23, which is vol. 18 of *The Collected Works of John Stuart Mill*. The quotation as given weaves together a full sentence by Mill with the quotation in brackets which precedes it by a few lines. The meaning is not altered. – Ed. of Hayek's works.]
4. [A. V. Dicey, *Lectures on the Relation Between Law & Public Opinion in England During the Nineteenth Century* (London: Macmillan, 1914). – Ed. of Hayek's works.]
5. [Adam Smith, *An Inquiry into the Nature and Causes of the Wealth of Nations* [1776], Book IV, Chapter ii, in *The Glasgow Edition of the Works and Correspondence of Adam Smith*, vol. 2:1 (Oxford: Clarendon Press, 1976), p. 471. – Ed. of Hayek's work.]
6. [This happened during a quiet period on the Italian front, on the Piave. The two books were by Grunzl and Jentsch. Hayek later told us, 'I still marvel that these particular books did not give me a permanent distaste for the subject.' – Ed. of Hayek's works.]
7. [The length of the usual undergraduate degree programme in Britain. – Ed. of Hayek's works.]
8. 'Students of social science must fear popular approval; evil is with them when all men speak well of them. If there is any set of opinions by the advocacy of which a newspaper can increase its sale, then the student … is bound to dwell on the limitations and defects and errors, if any, in that set of opinions: and never to advocate them unconditionally even in an *ad hoc* discussion. It is almost impossible for a student to be a true patriot and to have the reputation of being one at the same time.' – Alfred Marshall. [Quoted in A. C. Pigou, 'In Memoriam: Alfred Marshall', in

A. C. Pigou, *Memorials of Alfred Marshall* (New York: Kelley & Millman, 1956), p. 89. For more on Marshall's views of the duties of the economist see John K. Whitaker, 'Some Neglected Aspects of Alfred Marshall's Economic and Social Thought', *History of Political Economy*, vol. 9, no. 2 (Summer 1977), pp. 161–97, esp. pp. 185–90. – Ed. of Hayek's works.]

Recommended Works on the Economics Profession and on Being an Economist

Anderson, Martin 1992, 'The Glass Bead Game', Chapter 4 of his *Imposters in the Temple* (New York: Simon & Schuster), pp. 79–122.

Bauer, P. T. 1981. 'Reflections on the State of Economics', Chapter 15 in his *Equality, the Third World, and Economic Delusion* (Cambridge, Mass.: Harvard University Press), pp. 255–66.

Bauer, P.T. 1984. 'Further Reflections on the State of Economics', Chapter 10 of his *Reality and Rhetoric: Studies in the Economics of Development* (Cambridge: Harvard University Press), pp. 152–63.

Boettke, Peter J. 1996. 'What Is Wrong with Neoclassical Economics (And What Is Still Wrong with Austrian Economics)', in Fred Foldvary (ed.), *Beyond Neoclassical Economics* (Aldershot, England: Edward Elgar).

Boettke, Peter J. 1997. 'Where Did Economics Go Wrong? Modern Economics as a Flight from Reality', *Critical Review*, 11 (1), pp. 11–64.

Buchanan, James M. 1979. *What Should Economists Do?* (Indianapolis: Liberty Fund).

Cannan, Edwin 1933. 'The Need for Simpler Economics', *Economic Journal*, 43 (September), pp. 367–78.

Coase, Ronald H. 1975. 'Economists and Public Policy', in J. Fred Weston (ed.), *Large Corporations in a Changing Society* (New York: New York University Press) Reprinted in Coase's *Essays on Economics and Economists* (Chicago: University of Chicago Press, 1994), pp. 47–63, and in the present volume.

Colander, David 1991. *Why Aren't Economists As Important As Garbagemen? Essays on the State of Economics* (Armonk, NY: M. E. Sharpe).

Colander, David and Reuven Brenner (eds) 1992. *Educating Economists* (Ann Arbor, Mich.: University of Michigan Press).

Graham, Frank D. 1942. *Social Goals and the Economic Institutions* (Princeton, NJ: Princeton University Press). Selection (from pp. xv–xx) reprinted in the present volume.

Harberger, Arnold C. 1993. 'The Search for Relevance in Economics',

American Economic Review (Papers and Proceedings), May, 1–16.

Hayek, Friedrich A. 1944. 'On Being an Economist', an address given to economics students at the London School of Economics in 1944, first published in *The Trend of Economic Thinking: Essays on Political Economists and Economic History* (vol. III of *The Collected Works of F. A. Hayek*), edited by W. W. Bartley and Stephen Kresge (Chicago: University of Chicago Press, 1991), pp. 35–48. Reprinted in the present volume.

Hutt, William H. 1936. *Economists and the Public* (reprinted New Brunswick, NJ: Transaction Publishers, 1990). Selection (from pp. 34–7, 207–17) reprinted in the present volume.

Hutt, William H. 1971. *Politically Impossible ... ? An Essay on the Supposed Electoral Obstacles Impeding the Translation of Economic Analysis into Policy, or, Why Politicians Do Not Take Economic Advice* (London: Institute of Economic Affairs).

Kirzner, Israel M. 1983. 'Does Anyone Listen to Economists' (a review of George Stigler's *Economist As Preacher and Other Essays*), *Inquiry*, April, pp. 38–40. Reprinted with new title in the present volume.

Klamer, Arjo 1983. *Conversations with Economists* (Totowa, NJ: Rowman & Allanheld).

Klamer, Arjo and David Colander 1990. *The Making of An Economist* (Boulder, Col.: Westview Press).

Knight, Frank H. 1951. 'The Role of Principles in Economics and Politics' (Presidential address at the American Economics Association, 1950), *American Economic Review*, 41 (March) Reprinted in Knight's *On the History and Method of Economics* (Chicago: University of Chicago Press), pp. 251–81.

Leijonhufvud, Axel 1973. 'Life Among the Econ', *Western Economic Journal*, September, pp. 327–37.

Machovec, Frank M. 1995. *Perfect Competition and the Transformation of Economics* (New York: Routledge).

Mayer, Thomas 1993. *Truth Versus Precision in Economics* (Aldershot, England: Edward Elgar).

McCloskey, D. N. 1985. *The Rhetoric of Economics* (Madison: University of Wisconsin Press).

McCloskey, D. N. 1987. *The Writing of Economics* (New York: Macmillian).

McCloskey, D. N. 1994. *Knowledge and Persuasion in Economics* (New York: Cambride University Press).

McCloskey, D. N. 1996. *The Vices os Economists – The Virtues of the Bourgeoisie* (Amsterdam: Amsterdam University Press).

Philbrook, Clarence 1953. '"Realism" in Policy Espousal', *American Economic Review*, 43 (December), pp. 846–59. Reprinted in the present volume.

Schelling, Thomas C. 1995. 'What Do Economists Know?', *The American Economist*, 39 (Spring 1995), pp. 20–2. Reprinted in the present volume.

Summers, Lawrence H. 1991. 'The Scientific Illusion in Empirical Economics', *Scandinavian Journal of Economics*, 93(2), 27–39.

Tullock, Gordon 1984. 'How to Do Well While Doing Good!', an address delivered during the early 1970s at Virginia Polytechnic Institute. Published in David C. Colander (ed.), *Neoclassical Political Economy: The Analysis of Rent-Seeking and DUP Activities* (Cambridge, Mass.: Ballinger, 1984), pp. 229–40. Reprinted in the present volume.

Yeager, Leland B. 1997. 'Austrian Economics, Neoclassicism, and the Market Test', *Journal of Economic Perspectives* 11, 4 (Fall), 153–65.

Index of Names

About the Cato Institute

Founded in 1977, the Cato Institute is a public policy research foundation dedicated to broadening the parameters of policy debate to allow consideration of more options that are consistent with the traditional American principles of limited government, individual liberty, and peace. To that end, the Institute strives to achieve greater involvement of the intelligent, concerned lay public in questions of policy and the proper role of government.

The Institute is named for *Cato's Letters*, libertarian pamphlets that were widely read in the American Colonies in the early eighteenth century and played a major role in laying the philosophical foundation for the American Revolution.

Despite the achievement of the nation's Founders, today virtually no aspect of life is free from government encroachment. A pervasive intolerance for individual rights is shown by government's arbitrary intrusions into private economic transactions and its disregard for civil liberties.

To counter that trend, the Cato Institute undertakes an extensive publications program that addresses the complete spectrum of policy issues. Books, monographs, and shorter studies are commissioned to examine the federal budget, Social Security, regulation, military spending, international trade, and myriad other issues. Major policy conferences are held throughout the year, from which papers are published thrice yearly in the *Cato Journal*. The Institute also publishes the quarterly magazine *Regulation*.

In order to maintain its independence, the Cato Institute accepts no government funding. Contributions are received from foundations, corporations, and individuals, and other revenue is generated from the sale of publications. The Institute is a nonprofit, tax-exempt, educational foundation under Section 501(c)3 of the Internal Revenue Code.

Cato Institute, 1000 Massachusetts Ave., N.W.,Washington, DC, 20001